"Ashley is an incredible coach with a unique combination of expertise, honesty, vulnerability, and passion that will guide you through a journey of self-discovery to find out more about who you are and what is holding you back. Her authentic voice and presence shine through because she has been where you are and overcome the challenges that can feel too big to surmount. As a coaching client, I know firsthand that following this process will shake up the way that you think and help you see that there is a different, more fulfilling way to approach your career. Ashley helped me realize that, to do more than just find the next rung on the ladder, I needed to approach the process differently. She showed me how to do it, and I'm confident this book will do the same for you. Everyone should have Ashley's voice in their head as they move toward their career purpose, and this book means that you can."

— Elizabeth Ruth, MPP
Coaching client of the author

"This book is absolutely a must-read for anyone wanting to holistically approach their lifelong career journey! It very clearly walks the reader through how to begin emotionally preparing for a job search, discovering their career purpose, and then enacting on that purpose. This is an excellent and necessary companion book for any traditional job-search strategy. As a career coach for over ten years, I will be recommending this book to all of my friends, family, and clients!"

— Rhonda Sarmento, MA, psychology, and career coach
Boston Consulting Group

"If you are starting your career, transitioning, or making a life change, you must read Ashley Freeman's *The Path to Your Career Purpose*. I only wish that I had read it fifty years ago when I left college and started my Army career, or even when I was preparing to retire from the Army after thirty-eight years. I found the personal reflections and stories insightful and impactful in understanding the process of developing one's career purpose. As a veteran who coaches leaders transitioning from the Army and as a teacher working with MBA students who are looking for that next career, my advice is that this book is for you. Pick it up today!"

— P. K. (Ken) Keen
Lieutenant general, retired, U.S. Army
Associate dean for Leadership Development
Emory University Goizueta Business School

"EVERYONE needs to read *The Path to Your Career Purpose*. Ashley Freeman cracks the code on unlocking career purpose while providing relatable and actionable ideas for the reader, regardless of their phase of career exploration.

I loved the three-part process that inspired me to plan the best sequence of steps to find and live out my true career purpose. I can't wait to see how I can use these gems for the rest of my career.

I highly recommend it!"

— Ash Merchant, founder and CEO
Lionheart Partners, LLC

"This book is for any college student navigating their career. Ashley's universal text imparts authentic expertise about considering personal values to find more fulfillment in your career journey. Her concrete examples and in-text exercises give me the drive to keep pursuing my goals!"

— Christine Zhou
Undergraduate student

"Ashley Freeman possesses the unique ability to develop strategy at the highest levels within an organization and to also achieve the strategic goals by implementing the needed tactics and inspiring team members to contribute effectively and efficiently. Because of these abilities, Ashley is able to coach others to achieve more than they would otherwise ever accomplish. This book will be an invaluable gift to anyone who will agree to give strong consideration to Ashley's advice and make the enormous leap from merely accepting your current situation in life to pursuing a meaningful and fulfilling career. You will never regret the decision to achieve the most possible from your efforts, and to develop the relationships that will provide the foundation for all that you decide to pursue."

— Gary Teal, MBA
Vice president, Woodruff Health Sciences Center, Emory University
Chief of staff to the CEO and chairman of the board, Emory Healthcare

The Path to Your
CAREER PURPOSE

Find and Live
the Life of Fulfilling Work
You Were Meant to Do

ASHLEY S. FREEMAN

Publishing support provided by
Ignite Press
5070 N. Sixth St. #189
Fresno, CA 93710
www.IgnitePress.us

ISBN: 979-8-9855626-0-6
ISBN: 979-8-9855626-1-3 (Hardcover)
ISBN: 979-8-9855626-2-0 (E-book)

For bulk purchase and for booking, contact:

Ashley S. Freeman
Info@CareerPurposeBook.com
www.CareerPurposeBook.com

Library of Congress Control Number: 2021925910

Cover design by Anis El Idrissi
Edited by Emma Hatcher
Interior layout by Michelle White
Author photo by Stacie Renea Photography
Interior graphics by Martin Veleski

FIRST EDITION

To my dad, who brought out the fullest,
most authentic version of me and all those he knew.

May we all have someone in our life
who believes in us the way he would if he were here.

CONTENTS

FOREWORD

Dear reader, I am thrilled that you have begun a journey of self-discovery and a quest for your career purpose. Over the years, I've had the pleasure of teaching thousands of MBA students who were looking for more from their careers and in search of that elusive thing we call purpose. Some of my fondest memories come from those times in the classroom. One of the more unique sessions that I was asked to lead was a career-discovery session for incoming MBA students. This session always occurred during the students' orientation week, before they started their program, and was designed to help them further explore why they were getting an MBA, and more importantly, how they could best use the program to get them to where they wanted to go. For the students that were currently working (Evening MBA students, Executive MBA students, etc. . . .) this session was particularly eye-opening.

For these working students, I would kick off the session by informing the students that I was going to ask them to move to one of four "workplace satisfaction" corners in the room. I would then proceed to describe what each corner of the room represented and invite the students to self-select the corner that resonated with them most. Corner one was for all of the students that loved their job and loved their company. These students wanted to use the degree to accelerate down the path that they were on currently. They had found their workplace of a soulmate. Corner two was for the students that liked their job and company but were open to exploring other opportunities that an MBA degree might open up (think of this corner as comfortable with where they are but also open to casual dating). Corner three was for the students that either liked their job but did not like their company or liked their company but did not like their job. This group was actively looking to make a change. (Think of this group as either wanting to go to "couples counseling" to fix the relationship or looking to move on if things weren't going to improve. Regardless, change was imminent.) Corner four was for the students that neither liked their job nor liked their company. They were ready for a major life change and were planning on using the degree to facilitate that move immediately (think of this group as not only actively planning to end their current relationship but also in search of something).

When I was finished describing the corners, I would then announce to the room that they had just a few moments to move to that location that resonated with them the most. Imagine that there were eighty students in attendance in the session. Can you guess what the corners would look like when the students were finished selecting?

Here's how the exercise would typically play out: Corner one would have about four bubbly individuals, giddy about their respective jobs and companies. Corner two typically would have approximately eight students with a look of comfort on their faces, but with the occasional wandering eye. Corner three would typically have approximately twelve students, all ready to make a potential change, but each had something that she or he still wanted to hold onto. And then we would come to corner four. Bursting at the seams would be a group of over fifty students, who were ready to make a change starting today. Their energy and anxiety were palpable.

I would then describe what I was observing to the students and the true differences between the corners. As I would put it, the difference between corners one through four was a matter of "itchiness." The more itchy that each individual was in her or his current situation, the more they were drawn to the higher corners. And then I would go on to explain that the first step in any process of change was to acknowledge one's "itchiness." The second step was to identify how to scratch that itch, which can be a bit more complicated.

So, my dear reader, I pose the question to you:

"How itchy are you AND how ready are you to scratch that itch?"

I have a strong hunch that you resonate with those souls standing in corner four. Perhaps, you would be right there with them, given the chance. But, identifying that there is an itch is only the first step. Scratching the itch is much harder. It is a journey that requires a healthy dose of courage, a scaffolding built on faith, a strong will, and a clear purpose steering you true. It is an emotional journey as much as it is a logical one, with fear fighting you along the way.

No book or resource better captures the emotional challenge that accompanies living out one's true purpose than this book that you are currently in possession of.

Through the following pages, you will be equipped with "essentials" to help you not only find that place of career purpose and meaning but also the necessary tools to get you to that promised land. You will learn:

- What limiting beliefs and fears are holding you back.
- What your unique career purpose is that is waiting for you.
- How to prepare and pack for the journey ahead.
- How to overcome all the voices that try to keep you from realizing your true purpose and calling.

You've already begun the journey. If you follow the steps outlined in the pages ahead, you will most certainly see yourself moving closer to the life that you've always wanted.

Let's begin.

Brandon Smith, MS, MBA
"The Workplace Therapist"
Author, professor, podcaster, executive coach

PREFACE

I believe in a world in which we all live a life of meaningful and fulfilling work, and that the path to get there is not one that only a select few have the capacity to find, or the right to access. We are all unique; and therefore, we *all* have within us a unique combination of passions and talents to carry out those passions in the work that we do. Because of this, I find it utterly tragic that most people are not doing work that they love. What amazing gifts the world is missing out on! Further, because none of us knows how long we have left on this earth, I believe that a life in which we do work that we love is the only way to live—and that there is no time to waste going after it.

Over the last ten years, I have been on a journey to learn about myself, what my career purpose is, and how to make a full-time living at it. I have observed in my own career, and in that of almost everyone I know, how often we settle unnecessarily for work that we don't enjoy. And I have watched the consequences that ensue—everything from unrealized joy and potential to downright unhealthy stress levels. I will not pretend that it is easy to figure out what unique value we bring to the world and align it with the work that we do, but I will promise that the effort is worth it. After going after my own career purpose, I now get to do work every day that I absolutely *love* doing. I have the honor and privilege of helping people, as their coach and facilitator, to live better, more fulfilling lives—and it's the best job in the world. Why shouldn't you get to feel that way about your work, too? I have great news: you can! I wrote this book to help expedite the process for you by sharing the lessons I have learned on my own journey and from my clients' journeys. I consider it my purpose in life to help people reveal the fullest, most authentic versions of themselves into this world, and that's exactly what I hope this book does for you.

My worst nightmare for this book is for it to become a little inspirational book that lives on your coffee table. I did not write it to provide you with a smile when you occasionally pick it up, flip through it, set it back down, and resume life as usual. While I mean no disrespect to such "coffee table books," I did not write this book with the intention of it being one of them. I continued showing up to the keyboard to write, week after week, no matter what, so that your life could change—*actually change!*—for the better. Whether it's because one line makes you think differently about your path, or because having your career purpose in front of you means that you can no longer ignore what you're meant to do on this earth, it is my heart's desire that you experience positive, lasting transformation so that your life will never be the same after reading this book.

To this end, I have included ample detailed and practical tips for what to do at each step of the journey, as well as reflection questions to coach you through the process. The book is designed both for cover-to-cover reading that gives you an overview of the process and for how-to guidance as you complete each step. It will be important to keep moving through the process without stalling at any particular step. To do this, you could either read the book twice—first to get a feel for the process, and then to complete the exercises and questions—or you could keep your favorite note-taking tool handy so that you can keep track as you read and make notes of any exercises that you need to come back to.

Depending on where you are along your path, you may not need some sections; I tried to include the whole process for those who need it all. I also encourage you to keep an open mind while you read, as you may not yet understand why or how some parts apply to you, but if you have already completed some steps, or feel strongly that some do not resonate, you should feel free to focus only on the ones where you feel that you need the most guidance.

You may notice throughout the book that none of the real-world examples I provided have names associated with them. The reason I chose this approach is so that everyone can more directly relate to and feel included in the examples.

Although the word *career* appears in the title, this is not a book about how to find a job. Rather, it is meant to *complement* traditional job-searching strategies, such as crafting a résumé, practicing for behavioral interview questions, and developing an "elevator pitch." While these strategies are important components of the job-searching process, information about them is widely available. The goal of *this* book is to pick up where a career coach, mentor, or career-transition program might leave off. It will guide you on a journey to discover fulfilling work above and beyond a job that simply matches your background and skills, or one that represents the next step on a logical, prescribed path up the career trajectory from where you currently are. In fact, you don't even have to be in what we might typically think of as a "career" to use the core principles in this book. You can live a life of fulfilling work no matter what stage of life you are in, or whether you're on a traditional or nontraditional path.

Our journey together will be separated into three parts: first, we'll cover background information and foundations to clarify where you are now and what you need to do to set yourself up for success; second, we'll work through a method for clarifying what your career purpose and dream jobs are; and third, we'll review some tools to get you through the transition from where you are now to living your career purpose every day.

Before we dive in, I will offer one disclaimer: finding your career purpose is not a shortcut to—or the same thing as—happiness. We are probably all guilty at some point of thinking, "If I could just have [fill in the blank], then I would be happy." If you've inserted "my dream job" into that blank, I'll save you some time and offer gentle encouragement to consider whether there's another challenge in your life that you're hoping this process will "fix." If so, not to worry! You can certainly explore how to address other challenges *and* find your career purpose at the same time, as long as you're clear on the difference between them.

Now, reader, it's time to start our journey. As we begin, I want you to know that I believe in you. I believe you're meant for more, and I know deep down you believe that, too. You have the most amazing and unique set of gifts that nobody else in all of time—past, present, or future—will ever have. I know that there's room to reveal more of those gifts that you have inside you and to share more of them with the world around you. It's incredibly important work for you to do, because no one else can do it for you. I'll be here with you along the way to guide you through the process of unleashing the fullest, most authentic version of yourself, because the world needs you to be *you*. Let's find your career purpose!

Ashley S. Freeman
Atlanta, Georgia, United States of America
April 2022

PART I

BACKGROUND AND FOUNDATIONS

CHAPTER 1
WHERE YOU ARE AND
HOW YOU GOT HERE

"Everyone has his own specific vocation or mission in life;
everyone must carry out a concrete assignment
that demands fulfillment."
— *Viktor E. Frankl,* Man's Search for Meaning

"Y ou're literally killing yourself with the stress at work," your doctor tells you.

The words pierce right through you, and your heart sinks. "What kind of life am I living?" you wonder aloud. "When I'm gone, is *that* the story I would want people to tell about me—that I worked myself to death?" You consider brushing off the doctor's words—they were, after all, relatively extreme—but you can't lie to yourself anymore. You can't continue compromising your well-being, and your family's well-being, under the assumption that you must stay in your current situation indefinitely to make financial ends meet. In hearing this stark warning, you come to the realization that you are ready to face the truth: you've been making excuses to avoid the risky, the scary, and the unknown. You've told yourself it was better to stay with what you knew than to take a chance on a career change, or that you were too busy, or that you would do it later—or maybe even something deeper, such as you're not good enough or don't deserve work that would make you happy. You now see that the pride you took in working so hard was really just a rationalization for your behavior. With this newfound clarity, you finally admit to yourself that you've been living for the weekends, dreading Mondays, and neglecting to address the unhealthy habits you've formed along the way to distract you, all while making lighthearted jokes about it. And it has to change. Now.

You sit at your desk and stare blankly at a job search engine that you've opened on your computer as the sound of a clock ticks in the background. You have no idea what terms to begin searching, much less what your next career move could be if you were to leave this job that is deluging your life with stress. What in the world will you do? With a sigh of determination, you enter the first keywords that come to mind, which are just permutations on the job title you currently have. "Maybe it's a start," you think hopefully. You find little of interest and are tempted to give in—to go back to what you know—but you resolve to keep looking for clues.

The next day, everything changes. You're sitting at the same desk where you've been working for years, but this particular day, you start paying attention to how you *feel* as you go about your workday. You begin considering something that you hadn't previously: instead of focusing on what you're skilled at doing, you consider which activities and meetings excite you, and which ones you dread. You find yourself drawn to the office next door where the employees are working on a project that is related to what you do, but not part of your job description. "What is it about their work that is so interesting to me?" you wonder.

A few days later, a mass email finds its way to your email inbox and you feel strangely excited about it. It seems like it could be another clue. "Book Club," the subject touts. You don't particularly care for book clubs (aren't those for kids?), but this topic is intriguing. You decide to follow that feeling, too, and you attend the book club. Among like-minded readers, you just can't seem to get enough of the topic. You now want to read every book and attend every talk on this subject. You're hungry to understand it more. You have no idea at the time, but within about a year and a half, you would find yourself in a new role where you're applying these lessons.

The new role feels nothing short of magical. You find such joy in applying the lessons that you've been learning, and in seeing how they genuinely change lives for the better. Yet you still feel a yearning for even more—you've found something so powerful, you feel like you need to share it on a much broader scale. Determined, you seek and narrow some options for how you could go about sharing the message more broadly via different career paths within your industry, based on the same sort of "feelings compass" that you used to guide your initial steps in the journey. Eventually, you narrow the choices down to one—entrepreneurship—and you find the courage to leave this role to start a business that will share your new knowledge with as many people as you can for as long as you live.

*   *   *

Which parts of this story remind you of your own? At which point on this path do you find yourself located currently?

This story is based on my own journey. However, I would say it's actually all of our journeys.

Of course, not every detail applies universally. You may not have had a "wake-up call" moment like I had on the call with my doctor, but we are all guilty of "playing small" at some point in our lives and careers. Some of us avoid thinking about the risk that we would have to take or the fears we would have to face to go after the work that we're meant to do, so we take whatever job comes our way next. Some of us are settling for less than we know that we're capable of, simply "going through the motions" and paying the bills. Some have even made an active decision not to go after our dream job, despite knowing exactly what it is.

These are the stories of my clients, my loved ones, my colleagues, my acquaintances, and myself; they are all of our stories, and in that sense, they are the stories of being human. However, I bet you know at least one person who is in their dream job—perhaps you are even living vicariously through them now. Is there some special quality that they have that you don't? Is there something superhuman about them? Do they deserve more than you do? If we admit that the answer to these questions is *no*, the good news emerges: Finding your career purpose is not something that a chosen few get to experience. We *all* have the capacity to find and live a life of fulfilling work. The even better news is that you don't have to wait for a wake-up call to go after it—all you have to do is *decide* to do it, and this book will guide you from there.

> "Too many of us are not living our dreams because we are living our fears." — *Les Brown*

As you begin this journey, take a moment to reflect on what story you want people to tell about your life—do you want them to tell the version where you stayed "small," or the version where you went after your career purpose and gave the fullest version of yourself to the world? What will the world miss if you don't go after it? If your heart is telling you deep down that there is more that you could bring to the world, then it is no mistake that you are reading this book and that you are reading it now. You are right where you are meant to be, and now is your time to reveal to the world what you're on this earth to do—whether you're twenty or ninety years old, or somewhere in between.

WHAT IS A "CAREER PURPOSE?"

You may have heard of (or already done some work to identify) a *life* purpose, sometimes referred to as a personal mission. Your life purpose may include components such as who you are at your core, what your values are, why you feel you exist on this earth, and what ultimately matters most to you. But what about our professional lives, where we spend roughly 90,000 hours over the course of our lifetime?[1]

Spoiler alert: your career purpose is not fundamentally different than your life purpose, just as you do not somehow become a fundamentally different person when you go from work to home. *Your career purpose is simply the* **way** *in which you go about accomplishing your life purpose—or mission— through the work that you do.* And while this work is typically performed in exchange for income, if income is not a primary driver or need in your situation, then you still have a career purpose. (We'll address this in more detail in upcoming chapters.)

> Your career purpose is the way in which you go about accomplishing your life purpose through the work that you do.

You can carry out your career purpose in any number of industries or roles, because it is deep and broad in nature; it describes the meaning behind what you do rather than any specific role that you might have. In fact, it is the one thread that connects what you find meaningful about all the jobs that you have held along your path. While we all have preferences in our jobs that make them more or less enjoyable for us—tasks we enjoy more than others, people we prefer to work with, or environments in which we thrive—a career purpose provides something deeper than enjoyment or happiness. It is on another level entirely, one in which you find a sense of *fulfillment* in your work.

This fulfillment is what separates an interesting or fun job, or one that you're very skilled at doing, with one that provides a sense of purpose, alignment, and peace in your life. It gives you a sense that you are doing what you are *meant* to do on this earth. Going after your career purpose doesn't mean, of course, that every job along your path will be easy, or that you will enjoy all aspects of each job. Rather, the components of the job that you *do* enjoy will far outweigh any components that you don't. You will end a typical day with that sense of satisfaction and joy, no matter how hard you've worked or how tired you are.

It is also important to note that as you grow and change, your ideal job will too. That's why I use the broader term *career* when referring to your career purpose. Throughout this book, you'll also find the term *dream job*, which I use to refer to one *specific* job or role along your career purpose journey. When you find your dream job using the methodology in this book, you could find shortly thereafter that there's a particular aspect of it that you want to dive more deeply into, or a higher-level role that you'd like to seek along the same path, or a change in what you want to do based on new insights that you've gained—and thus, your dream job will change as you grow. Because your career purpose is a journey more than a destination, embarking on the journey is simply a commitment to keep moving forward along the path.

> Because your career purpose is a journey more than a destination, embarking on the journey is simply a commitment to keep moving forward along the path.

What about you? What does the idea of "career purpose" mean to you? Before you continue, pause for a moment and make a note of your answer to this question somewhere where you can look back at it later. You might include whatever you pictured when you read the title of this book—what did you envision that you'd get out of reading a book about the path to your career purpose?

If you're not sure where to start, here are some real-life examples from my clients to give you some ideas:

- A sense of alignment between my work life and home life
- A passion, not just a means to an income
- A way to use my gifts in service to others
- Building a professional legacy
- Loving what I do and with whom I work
- Aligning my hobbies with my day job
- A career that really *means* something
- Overarching clarity and intention in my career

A broad and basic jot list of characteristics like this is fine for now; we'll develop the ideas later on. Keep in mind that the point of this question is to identify your *own* definition. You'll want to review it throughout the process—to remind yourself where you're going—and also when you get to your dream job, so that you know when you've arrived.

Now that you have an idea of what a career purpose is and what it means to you, you may be wondering where this idea came from. To seek a sense of purpose in life is to be human, and in that sense, you could say the idea of purpose in our work has always existed on some level. However, the idea that work could be a source of meaning, and not just a means to generate income, seems to be a relatively new (or newly accepted) concept. Why is this?

HOW WE GOT HERE: A BRIEF HISTORICAL NOTE

"The way I was raised, 'because I said so' was a good enough reason," one of the leaders I coached told me. "These younger employees I manage just don't seem to get it. Why should I have to explain *why?*"

He had been working at the company for most of his career, nearly forty years. He was nearing retirement, as were several of his direct reports. They had grown up in a world in which the organization returned the loyalty of its employees and took care of them for the duration of their career. The employees, in return, were grateful for this care, felt a sense of pride in their work, and didn't ask questions like "why." One Baby Boomer I spoke with recounted: "It was honorable to stay at an organization your whole career. Longevity meant something—employers *wanted* people to work there a long time, because they valued the knowledge that these employees gained over time." You could argue, then, that the sense of meaning came at least in part from the employer-employee relationship.

Then came the rise of the principle of shareholder primacy—which asserts that the only legitimate purpose of a corporation is to maximize value for its shareholders—in the late 1970s and early 1980s. While any judgements about the merits of this principle are outside the scope of this book, I wanted to mention it because it seems only natural that a shift toward prioritizing shareholders, profit, and quarterly earnings would also result in a fundamental shift in the dynamic between the organization and its employees.[2]

You can call the relatively new focus on career purpose "generational" if you'd like, because as many children of Baby Boomers watched their parents (or their friends' parents) get laid off as a result of this shift in priorities, it provided a new opportunity to find one's own sense of meaning in work. It would only make sense that if employees couldn't count on having a job the next day, then they would want to seek a purpose (a "why") for their work, something bigger than themselves. More recently, the effects of the COVID-19 pandemic on the workplace seemed to bring greater attention to this dynamic via a higher quit rate than usual in most industries, a trend termed "The Great Resignation." Without going into great detail, it's worth noting that factors such as job insecurity and employees prioritizing what really matters (and reevaluating their work accordingly) are considered to be among the aspects that contributed to this trend.[3,4,5]

By all means, we are incredibly blessed when we have jobs, and we should be grateful for the ability to put food on the table and pay our bills. My point is not to lay blame or suggest that anyone not take the relationship with their employer seriously; besides, many organizations take great care of their people, and, as we conduct our job search, we can prioritize working for those types of organizations. My point is simply that, as the workplace dynamic shifted, we now each have the opportunity, the ability, and even the responsibility for finding a sense of meaning in our work—for finding and living our career purpose. Now, let's find yours.

"YOU ARE HERE": DEFINING WHERE YOU ARE CURRENTLY ON THE PATH

What is your starting point on the journey to find and live your career purpose? We all are at different stages, and there is no "correct" or "best" place to start other than where you are in this moment. To help you identify where you currently are, here are three descriptions of the most common scenarios that I've come across with my clients. As you read them, think about which one (or parts of one) you relate to the most:

You don't know what your dream job would be or haven't put much thought into it

Perhaps you've been chugging along in your career, getting promotions along the way, and following a fairly standard career trajectory. If you're on the earlier end of the path, maybe you've explored internships but aren't sure where to go next. You may like some aspects of the work you've done, but you don't know what would make it that much better—whether colleagues, company, industry, culture, environment, or something else. Perhaps you've never put much effort into exploring who *you* are and what you like. Either way, you've never really thought hard about a "dream" job; besides, they wouldn't call it *work* if it were supposed to be fun, right? You show up, do a good job, and do your best to enjoy the time when you're not working. Maybe you even find yourself "surviving" until Fridays and dreading Mondays—and finding the humor in it all to help you keep going—while convincing yourself that you should just be grateful you have a job and do what they're paying you to do without complaining.

You know what your dream job is but have decided not to go after it

If you're in this group, you know what your dream job is, but have made a decision (whether consciously or not) to close off the path to get there. You may have had any number of reasons for making this decision: It may have seemed too good to be true, or too hard to make it happen, or too costly—financially or otherwise—or too late because of your age, or you've already invested too much in another path to change at this point, or you couldn't make enough income in that line of work to support your family. Those in this group tend to have a little voice inside that they've learned to quiet, but it keeps nagging them to varying degrees, insisting that they're meant for more.

You know what your dream job is and want to go after it but are afraid to make the leap

Enter the most common reason people come to me for help in this area: you know exactly what you want to do, and what it will take to get there, but you are afraid, nervous, or hesitant to do it. Whether you want to be an entrepreneur and have to quit your job to get started, or change industries and take a pay cut, or you have a great opportunity but don't feel qualified or ready for it, or you have to start over completely, this leap of faith into the unknown is terrifying. Trust me, I understand—I've been there (twice!), having to quit a "stable" job to get to my dream job. (I put "stable" in quotation marks because, as the COVID-19 pandemic taught us, few jobs are truly stable. When all your income comes from one source, that means it can also all be gone at once, whether through reorganization, downsizing, lay-offs, rapid shift in demand, recession, etc.). If you're in this group, you may have been putting off next steps, distracting yourself from taking action, or rationalizing why you should delay. You may have created a pros and cons list, sought advice, or otherwise begun putting plans into motion—in short, you may have done everything *but* go after it—because something keeps stopping you short of taking the "real" leap.

What about you? Which of these descriptions, or components of them, resonate with you? In what ways is your situation different? Take a moment to reflect, jot down, or discuss with a loved one where you are on your path currently. Clarity is key here—it's more difficult to see where to go if you aren't sure where you're starting.

WHY YOU HAVEN'T ACTED YET

Now that you know where you are on the path, let's uncover why you are where you are. Why haven't you gone after your career purpose yet?

When I saw the three scenarios in the previous section laid out at a high level for the first time, I remember sitting back in my chair with a little gasp, as my eyes opened wider. It had suddenly hit me: *What holds us back from going after our career purpose is our limiting beliefs, fears, and the stories we tell ourselves to rationalize avoiding them.* It is not the logistical challenges, or some old injury that we have, or lack of time or skill, or whatever we're telling ourselves that it is, that has kept us from going after

> What holds us back from going after our career purpose is our limiting beliefs, fears, and the stories we tell ourselves to rationalize avoiding them.

it. Those are actually examples of rationalizations (or "excuses," as we'll call them in chapter three when we dive deeper into this topic) that we make to avoid facing our fears.

Your openness to exploring this truth in your own journey is the key to unlocking your ability to move forward; it is the difference between this book serving as the momentary inspiration on your coffee table that I mentioned in the preface, or it serving as a catalyst for life-changing action.

If you're not yet convinced about my conclusion, let's take a look at those scenarios again.

To those who haven't tried to figure out what your dream job is (unless you've just started out in your career or recently transitioned out of military service—in which case, please know that there is no rush): Could you possibly be *putting off* the search, whether consciously or subconsciously? Could you be telling yourself deep down that you don't deserve your dream job, or that you don't have enough degrees, experience, etc., or that you should just be grateful for what you have, or that your career purpose will find *you* if you just work hard enough, or that your dream job doesn't fit what you think your loved ones or society expect of you? Are there other reasons that you haven't looked for your dream job (or haven't looked in the right places)? Could these reasons actually be rooted in fears or limiting beliefs—and if so, what might the *real* story be, not the one that you've been telling yourself?

To those who decided not to go after your dream job: What justification did you give for your decision? As I write this, I am thinking of two people I know personally in this category who declared to me that they cannot go after their dream job because they need to provide for their family, and they decided they couldn't make enough money at their dream job to do so. This is heartbreaking to me. No doubt, it is important to take care of our family, but what quality of life might you be providing if you are unhappy for a prolonged period in a job you're not meant to do? What might you risk teaching them by staying small and not living your dreams—if you take a "back seat" to life indefinitely and just pay the bills? What if, with time and effort, you could have *both* the financial stability to provide for your

"Disguising fear as a virtue [such as humility] is a convenient way to avoid feeling the pain of not having stepped fully into your life." – *Cory Muscara*

family *and* your dream job (not that it would necessarily be easy to figure out how—but is it *possible*)?

Perhaps your justification is that you want to keep the comforts and perceived happiness that the income is buying you, or you have convinced yourself that you or your family "need" these extra comforts that go beyond basic necessities. If so, I would ask: do you *really* need them? Is the money *really* buying comfort, well-being, or happiness? Do you believe that people who make a lower salary than you are necessarily less happy? Or, if you're living paycheck to paycheck or have significant debt, are these necessarily indefinite situations?

Whatever your justification is for not going after your dream job, I encourage you to ask yourself if you *truly* believe it deep down, or if there could be another, deeper belief or fear that you may have been avoiding.

To those in the final group, who are experiencing the granddaddy of all career purpose fears (the leap into the unknown): the fear that you feel is an understandable and natural human characteristic designed to protect us, and it certainly can keep us safer sometimes. However, is it serving you well in your current situation? Is any job truly as "stable" as we tell ourselves it is? What might you *really* be holding onto by not going after your career purpose—could it be perceived stability, what you know, or what you're more comfortable with? What might you discover that you're actually afraid of, if only you gave yourself permission to be honest or to reflect more deeply about it than you previously have—and how might this knowledge allow you to move past it?

> "Until you make the unconscious conscious, it will direct your life and you will call it fate." – *Carl Jung*

What about you? Take a moment to continue reflecting on any beliefs or fears that may have been holding you back so far. You may find it easier to do a quick search online for a list of limiting beliefs to give you something to react to instead of coming up with them from scratch; the most common ones that I have encountered are some variation of "I am not enough" (manifesting as "I'm not worthy"; "I don't have what I need"; "I don't deserve it"; "I don't have what it takes"; and so forth). Again, it's difficult to see where to go if you don't know where you are—and if you're going to find your career purpose, you'll have to shine a light on these beliefs before you can begin to move past them.

If you feel a sense of resistance or defensiveness to these ideas, that's okay too; it may help to start there, by reflecting on where those reactions are coming from.

Next, try focusing your thoughts on what you *do* want to happen instead of what you don't want to (or are afraid might) happen. One of my coaching clients found it helpful to create a list of limiting beliefs that she resonated with and then add a specific, positive response to each of them. For example: If one of your limiting beliefs is; "I will get it wrong," then a response could be, "I will figure this out because I have support and I'm persistent." To generate positive responses, you could ask yourself what you would say to someone else if they told you they believed that limiting idea about themselves.

* * *

Now that we see the underlying truth behind our actions (or inaction) and have revealed how we can all be held back by them to varying degrees, we can have peace of mind knowing that it is totally normal to have limiting beliefs and fears. The question is: Now that you have begun to shed more light on them, will you continue to let them hold you back? Will you choose to believe the voice deep inside, telling you that you're not enough, that you don't deserve success, that you won't make it, that you're too afraid, that you won't make enough money, or whatever lie it's telling you?

If you find through this process that you've been telling yourself stories and living anything less than the life that you're meant for, fear not—this is your time, and I promise you that there is light ahead! Right now, our goal is simply to recognize what has been holding us back; we will explore how to overcome these beliefs more in chapter seven.

> "Courage is not the lack of fear. It is acting in spite of it." — *Mark Twain*

You *can* find your career purpose no matter what's in your way; moreover, you can—and you *will*—overcome these obstacles, if you decide to do so.

Note: I want to acknowledge that delving into limiting beliefs and fears may be difficult for some, and that this process might make us feel less competent or secure at first. It is therefore a necessary part of the process to give yourself ample compassion and grace. These fears and beliefs served a purpose—to protect you and keep you going—and in exposing them for what they are, you can now give yourself permission to thank them and move in a different, healthier direction. If you are struggling with these ideas, do not hesitate to seek the advice of a loved one or licensed professional to help you process anything difficult that arises for you. You could also skip ahead to chapter seven for a few strategies to try. Finding your career purpose is not an easy or purely rational path; otherwise, you likely would have already completed the journey. Therefore, please know that any difficult emotions that you may find here are a sign that you're beginning the exact work that you need to do in order to move past them to find your career purpose.

*I also want to be very clear that if you haven't gone after your career purpose yet, or if your attempts haven't been successful, this is not somehow your "fault" or something that you did wrong. Your journey thus far happened the way that it did for a reason, just as this book has entered your path at this particular point in time for a reason. You are in exactly the right place, and everything that you have been through up until this point has been preparing you. Regardless of your age or stage of career, it is absolutely **never** too late to live a life of fulfilling work.*

WHY YOU SHOULD GO AFTER YOUR CAREER PURPOSE

You've hopefully now been able to put language around one or more limiting beliefs that have been holding you back from progressing on the path to finding your career purpose. They may be uncomfortable to think about, but simply recognizing that they are there is a *huge* first step! Now, because they are there for a reason—perhaps they made you feel secure by keeping you from taking risks—it may be tempting to want to hold onto them. You may have been operating with them for a long time. Why do anything about them now?

In Susan Cain's *New York Times* best-selling book, *Quiet: The Power of Introverts in a World That Can't Stop Talking,* she recounts a story by Mark Twain. In the story, a man traveled to heaven in search of the greatest general of all time who had passed away. When Saint Peter pointed the man to an "average Joe," the man argued, based on his experience of this person, that he was not in fact the greatest general of all time when they lived on Earth together. Cain writes, " 'I know that,' said Saint Peter, 'but if he *had* been a general, he would have been the greatest of them all.' "[6]

I have to choke back tears when I read that last line! Call me sensitive if you want, but to me, it is tragic to think of your story ending similarly. Whether or not you believe in heaven or saints, or whether we can all be the "greatest" at something, is beside the point here. What matters is preventing the *tragedy* of the world missing out on your gifts if you live life just "going through the motions," never going after your career purpose.

In case you need more reasons to embark on this journey, here are a few for your consideration:

You are the author in full control of your story

Is your current story the one that you want people to tell about your life when you leave this earth? You have full authority and ability to write any story that you choose, and if you don't, someone else (your boss, your family, "fate," etc.) could write the story for you. There will *always* be some reason not to go after what you really want in life. What story will you write for your life?

> What story will you write for your life?

Life is too short to live anything other than your purpose

The reality is that none of us knows whether we will be here one more day or a lifetime of more days. I learned this the hard way at age nineteen, when my father passed away suddenly. He was at the office on a Wednesday and gone by Sunday that same week. It's not a story that I talk about much, nor a reality that any of us wants to face about ourselves, but the fact is that a shortened lifespan can happen to anyone. We all know this on the surface level, but do you really *feel* the weight of the fact that you don't know how long your life will be? Given that reality, can you afford to spend time ignoring any voice or feeling inside you suggesting that there is more to your story?

You and your loved ones will live better lives

In his *Harvard Business Review* article "Manage Your Energy, Not Your Time," author Tony Schwartz encourages us that "If the work [people are] doing really matters to them, they typically feel more positive energy, focus better, and demonstrate greater perseverance." When you love what you do, not only will your work itself improve, but you will have greater energy and satisfaction. We all have the opportunity to bring *that* home to our friends and family rather than any stress, frustration, or burnout that we may be experiencing—and to be more fully present when we interact with them. How much more might you and your loved ones stand to thrive when you are able to show up more fully for them?[7]

You will live longer and be healthier along the way

A 2019 study of nearly 7,000 adults over the age of fifty found that a stronger sense of purpose in life was significantly associated with decreased all-cause mortality. That means the participants who scored the highest on a "life purpose" scale were less likely to die during the study period than those who scored lower. Whoa. There is a growing body of research in this area if you want to know more about *how* a sense of purpose affects us, but it's not rocket science (you're more likely to take care of yourself, you'll have less stress and inflammation, and so on). I don't know about you, but I'd much rather live the purposeful, healthier, and longer life![8,9]

You will be proud looking back on your life

When you look back on your life one day, will you be proud of the choices that you made, or might you regret not taking more risk to do what you love? Will you feel that you've done everything that you could to live your best life and use your talents, or might you find that you let fear or busyness get in the way? In choosing to go after your career purpose, you have the opportunity to feel proud and peaceful that you lived the life you were meant to live.

You deserve it!

Human beings are nothing short of incredible. We have developed amazing new technologies, advanced civilizations, cures for diseases, and the ability to travel to outer space. We are at the top of the food chain, have complex emotions, and are capable of intellectual achievements beyond any other species. You, reader, are a unique and wonderful part of the human species. This reality begs the question: who are you *not* to go after your purpose?

> "The best time to plant a tree was 20 years ago. The second best time is now."
> — *Chinese Proverb*

You'll inspire others and set an example

I was truly surprised by how much it inspired others when I began taking terrifying steps (like quitting my job) to go after my career purpose. I was so caught up in the fear that I was feeling that I didn't realize others perceived me as courageous until they started telling me how what I was doing made them think about making positive changes in their lives. Similarly, I had a coaching client one time whose younger sister was as afraid as my client was to go after her dream job. I asked my client, "What effect might it have on your sister's story if *you* don't go after your dream job?"

This is the opportunity waiting for all of us: In taking the scary steps first, we show those around us that they can, too. Conversely, when we limit ourselves from living our best lives, we can risk encouraging others around us to do the same by example. We may teach those we mentor, our families, our children, our direct reports, our friends, and our colleagues that it's okay to live status quo. We may even normalize and elevate settling for just being grateful for what we have (while struggling long term in a job that is the wrong fit) and sharing jokes about how slowly the time goes by when we're at work or how much we hate Mondays. If you relate, I want to encourage you that you are a magnificent human being who is meant for—and deserves— so much more than that. You weren't born to pay the bills and die!

There's only one of you in all of time

Most important of all the reasons is that the world has everything to lose if you don't go after your career purpose. If you don't share your unique set of talents and passions that nobody else will ever have, then nobody else ever can or will do it for you. The world *needs* you to do this work!

*   *   *

So, what will your story be? If you know you're meant for more, let's take a look at all the excitement that is in store for you when you get into your dream job.

A SNEAK PEEK INTO YOUR FUTURE

You wake up in the morning and think about what is on your calendar with a sense of excitement. "I can't believe that I get paid to do this," you think to yourself, shaking your head in disbelief. You've scheduled your day in the way you prefer, because you've done the work to find a job that honors whether you like structure or flexibility. Throughout the day, you engage in activities that give you a sense of fulfillment. Of course, there are some things you like more than others, just like in any job—but you feel a sense of freedom knowing that you are doing work that merges your skills and passions. Everything in your life is pointed in the same direction—as if all aspects of you are in alignment—and because of this, decisions and clarity come more naturally than they ever have. The peaceful feeling of alignment is indescribable, as if you realize that throughout your whole career you've been breathing smoky air and suddenly find yourself atop a mountain surrounded by the purest air that exists. Particularly if you've been in a toxic or unhealthy job previously, the grass now seems greener, the air clearer, and the sky bluer—you feel alive and free! You don't care if you have longer commute times, a tighter budget, or other inconveniences, because the work is overall so enjoyable that it seems to "cancel out" any frustrations you experience.

At lunch, you reflect on how you used to do work that you found fulfilling—maybe a "side gig"—on nights and weekends, just to feel some sense of fulfillment in your work. You think about tonight's plans, feeling grateful that you feel freer to enjoy life and no longer need to do extra work to get that sense of fulfillment because your day job now provides that. When people ask you what you do for a living, you answer with your role and add "... and it's the best job in the world." This particular day, you've just come back from vacation, and you mention in passing to a colleague that you have seven meetings. "You poor thing!" they say, "Seven meetings the day after a vacation?" With a grin, you respond: "Good thing I love what I do." People often tell you that your enthusiasm for what you do is infectious.

When the meetings are over and action items completed, you face one of your greatest challenges—not wanting to *stop* working—because, for you, work and play are now the same thing. Because the tension between bill-paying and enjoyable work has vanished, the colleagues and clients you work with experience a richer and more present version of you. Your talents and passions can shine, which enable a successful day naturally. You decide it's time to wrap up, perhaps tired from working hard, but the *best* kind of tired in which you know you served the world in exactly the way you were put on this earth to do. The effortless flow and exchange of energy from your day leaves you motivated and excited to see what's in store for you tomorrow.

What about you? How did you feel reading this description? It's not just a dream scenario I concocted—it is a compilation of actual quotes from real people I know who are in their dream jobs. If they can get there, so can you. Are you ready to tell someone this is the kind of day you've had? Let's get you there as soon as possible!

Which components of this description resonate with you? How might your ideal day in your dream job look similar or different? (Notice the word *ideal*—obviously, not every day will be an ideal one, no matter what work you're doing, but this visual gives us a clearer direction to work toward.) Start by taking a look back at the notes you wrote at the beginning of this chapter about what a career purpose means to you. The next step we'll take is very important, which is to make this visual much more specific and palpable to you. This is important because it's hard to go after something if you're not clear what it is, and also because the more clearly that you can picture it now, the more motivated that you'll be.

> The more clearly that you can picture your future, the more motivated you'll be to go after it.

To illustrate what I mean, pause and think about what you're going to have for your next meal. Go ahead—think of an answer before you read the next sentence. I'll wait.

If you pictured a vague idea, such as "I don't know, maybe something with the chicken in the freezer," then the meal is likely less appealing because your brain has to fill in a lot of detail. For example, how would you cook it—fry, pan sear, bake? What side items will you prepare to go with it? What sauces or seasonings will you use? However, if you pictured a specific dish in detail—such as your favorite dish at a local restaurant, or your mom's famous recipe—your mouth is probably watering in anticipation of the specific flavors and textures of that particular dish, because you know exactly what's coming.

Now, let's add some detail to your idea of living your career purpose to get your proverbial mouth watering. Don't worry if you don't know all the pieces right now; just get as detailed as you can. Some example questions to consider include: what kinds of people do you work with? How does your day flow? How do you start and end your day? Where do you envision doing the work and what does it look like there? How do you interact with people?

What do you notice with your five senses (tasting coffee, smelling fresh air, hearing a buzz of activity around you, feeling a comfy chair beneath you, seeing mountains in the background . . .)? What will it *feel* like to do fulfilling work? What excites you the most about this description? There are no right or wrong answers here; the goal for now is to get a vision and some feelings into your notes—talk it out with a loved one first if you prefer, but still write it down—so that you can begin feeling and anticipating it. In chapter four, we'll talk about how to process this information further.

HOW DO YOU KNOW IF YOU'RE READY?

Throughout our journey so far, we have examined what a career purpose is, where you are on the path to finding yours, what's been holding you back, why you should act, and what the future looks like for you when you do. No matter how excited you feel at the prospect of finding your career purpose, at some point, any fear and doubt that has held you back thus far may creep back in. "Do I have what it takes? Am I enough? Am I ready?" you might wonder.

I have some good news: You already have everything within you—*everything*—that you need to find and live your career purpose. You don't need anything else.

I'll say that louder for the folks in the back.

You have everything it takes to find and live your career purpose. You are already enough. You were born enough.

Now, there's a difference between having what it takes (or being capable) and being ready. You already have the former, and the latter is up to you.

> You have everything it takes to find and live your career purpose.

Ask yourself right now—no messing around—do you believe me? Are you going to go after your career purpose and commit not to rationalize why you shouldn't?

If the answer is yes, and you're still reading, it means that you're ready. Whether you're skimming to see if you want to embark on the journey, or you've made the commitment to read cover-to-cover, whatever subconscious beliefs have held you back from finding and living your career purpose up until this point likely would have otherwise kept you from reading the book. I'm not writing this book to convince people to read it—the people in that group are not ready yet. Because you are reading this, it means that at least part of you is open to what it has to say, and that's all you need.

As we'll explore in upcoming chapters, this pursuit is not primarily a logical or skill-based one; it is an emotional one. That means if you have feelings, then you can find your career purpose.

Yes, reader, you *are* ready. This is your time to shine.

CHAPTER 2
HOW TO SET YOURSELF UP FOR SUCCESS

"You can't do it alone. So don't pretend you can."
— *Simon Sinek,* Together Is Better

The decision to move to the next step on the path to your career purpose is a moment worth celebrating! Take a photo, make a note in a journal, or have a beverage with friends so that you can look back on this time when you're in your initial dream job.

Now, fasten your seat belt. You may have to take my word at this point when I say that it may be a wilder or longer ride than you expect, but those who make the journey say that it is worth every bit of it.

You may have seen a taste in the last chapter of why it is necessary to dedicate an entire chapter just to setting yourself up for success. Such a chapter would likely not be necessary for a book on standard job searching strategy, but going on the journey to find your career purpose can require some deeper work. My goal here is to ensure that, as you embark on this journey, you have the most supportive environment possible to help you through any obstacles you encounter so that you can thrive along the path.

Throughout this chapter, we will review several aspects of a supportive foundation, but it is not intended to be an exhaustive or be-all-end-all list. What's important is that you proactively build a sturdy foundation to set yourself up for success, and the ideas in this chapter will help you think through what can make it the best possible foundation for you.

What about you? Each of us is unique, which means we each have a unique set of needs for this journey. What are yours? Before you dive in, take a moment to jot down a few ideas for what you know to be true in your situation. Ask yourself: what does success on this career purpose journey mean to you? Deep down, what do you know you need in order to be successful? What factors have created success for you in the past? What do you need more (or less) of right now to help you on this path? Once you have a couple of ideas, it's time to build your foundation.

FOUNDATION #1: ENHANCE YOUR PHYSICAL SURROUNDINGS

In the 2011 movie *Limitless,* the main character, Eddie Morra, takes a pill that allows him to access the full capacity of his brain and makes his IQ soar to four digits. After taking the pill, he suddenly has the clarity to know exactly what he needs to do and how to do it. He remembers everything that he's ever seen or learned, and he makes instantaneous, effortless connections between all of these pieces of information. Let's pause there for a second. If you were in this situation, what would be the *first* thing you did when you arrived home with your newfound abilities? Finish a book that was previously too hard for you to follow? Learn a new skill? Enter a trivia contest?

If you've seen the movie, you may remember what happened: the first thing Eddie does upon entering his home is clean and declutter his environment. This scene provokes an interesting question: why would someone with access to their full brain capacity care about the quality of their physical surroundings? What does this character know that we stand to learn about how our environment could be holding us back?

While the story is obviously fictional, neuroscience backs up the idea that the more clutter we have in our environment, the harder our brain has to work to process it, and the more trouble we have functioning. (Mental "clutter" affects us similarly, but since we are focusing on our physical environment in this section, I'll simply recommend my favorite book for how to release the clutter we hold in our minds and free our capacity for having ideas: *Getting Things Done: The Art of Stress-Free Productivity* by David Allen.)[10,11]

It's not just the clutter that affects us. Aspects of our environment as simple as how bright the lights are can influence our mood and sleep. One report from 2004 even found more than 600 credible studies that showed how a number of different aspects of design in hospitals—from noise level, to ventilation, to ergonomic design—affect both medical outcomes for patients *and* the health and well-being of the hospital staff![12,13]

What about you? Take a look around wherever you are reading this right now. What do you notice with each of your five senses? How does what you notice make you feel? Perhaps you're in a coffee shop, enjoying tasty coffee and pleasant aromas, and the loud conversation next to you is making it frustrating to concentrate on reading. Maybe you're at home, and as you look up, you see several reminders of things that you need to do, like laundry, cleaning, maintenance, picking up the kids, or that call you need to make, and feel a little overwhelmed. Or perhaps you're out in nature, feeling the fresh air against your skin as you smell nearby plants and hear overhead birds chirping, and feel refreshed.

These inputs are all having an effect on us, usually without us being aware, which means that these inputs from our environment will either take up vital mental resources and drain us, or they will feed us with positive messages and energy. If you've ever noticed a difference in your energy and clarity levels when you made your bed, cleaned out a drawer, let some light in the room, or added a plant or positive quote to your workspace, then you know what I mean. The good news is this means that, while there are some aspects of our environment outside of our control, there are plenty of ways that we can proactively add positive influences in our surroundings to set us up for success.[14]

> What is your environment subliminally communicating to *your* brain?

What is your environment subliminally communicating to *your* brain? Is it full of powerful messages, clean surfaces, bright colors, or inspirational quotes and photos to tell you what a rockstar you are—fully prepared and excited for this journey? Which two or three aspects can you update about your environment to spur a more positive and successful mindset? What distractions or negative influences can you remove? Why wait? Go ahead and make a few positive tweaks now!

FOUNDATION #2: ALLOCATE MORE OF YOUR TIME AND ENERGY TO YOUR SUPPORTERS

Have you ever noticed a particular type of question in a follow-up email or customer survey you've received that reads something along the lines of "How likely are you to recommend this product, service, or company to a friend, on a scale of 1 to 10?" Your answer to this question reveals your Net Promoter Score (NPS), which measures your loyalty as a customer. First developed by Bain and Company in 2003, these ratings put customers into one of three categories: promoters, who give a score of 9 or 10 and are typically enthusiastic and loyal; passives, who give a score of 7 or 8 and are satisfied but not enough to talk about the brand to others; and detractors, who give a score of 0 to 6 and may actively talk negatively about the brand to their friends or colleagues.[15]

So, what does NPS have to do with you and your career purpose? Think of yourself like the company trying to measure customer loyalty, and think of the people you know as those filling out the survey. Those in your life who would fall in the promoter category (we'll call them your "supporters") are the ones you need to surround yourself with if you want to be successful on this journey. Likewise, you'll also want to be intentional about how and when you interact with those who would fall in the detractor category (we'll call them "naysayers"). What's important here is not to judge, but to be clear and to challenge any biases that might come into play, such as how close you are to them or who you think *should* be a supporter.

Before you run off to give all your friends an NPS survey (which I do not recommend, as it was not designed for that purpose!), here are a few ways that you can identify your supporters and naysayers as well as how to interact with each group during this process.

Who are your supporters?

Consider the following questions: If you called in the middle of the night with a ridiculous idea—such as going after your secret dream job of becoming a professional circus trainer—who would pick up the phone? After rubbing their eyes and wondering if you've lost your mind, who would respond with some combination of excitement for you and asking how they could help you?

Make a list of as many people as you can think of who come to mind who would respond this way. To make sure that your list is complete, it may help to consider all areas of your life: people from any schools that you've attended (including childhood friends), current and former colleagues, mentors, friends, family, extended family, those who follow you on social media, people to whom you've recently sent text messages, people from religious or neighborhood communities, those you've volunteered with, and so on. (If your list still feels short, not to worry—we'll talk about how to grow it momentarily.)

These are the people who will believe in you no matter what, who will support you no matter what crazy ideas you have, and who will remind you of the truth about you on the harder days. Therefore, *allocating more of your time and energy to your supporters is a non-negotiable prerequisite for finding your career purpose.* Because they are so critical to the process, your supporters will play a role throughout this book. As the opening quote for this chapter reminds us, the simple truth is that we need each other. Yes, even the most introverted or independent among us.

> Allocating more of your time and energy to your supporters is a non-negotiable prerequisite for finding your career purpose.

One final tip that I'll offer is that your list of supporters should not be confused with your inner circle of immediate friends and family. They may not be actively *un*supportive of you, and it certainly doesn't mean that they don't care about you if their name doesn't appear on your list, but they might simply not be interested in your industry, feel insecure about their own situation, or be otherwise occupied with something that is consuming their time.

Who are your naysayers?

You may not have any naysayers, but if you do, you'll know who they are. Like the detractors of the NPS, your naysayers have a negative attitude toward your new path as you begin changing, going after your career purpose, and flourishing. Their reactions to you could vary widely from a warning such as "I don't think that's a good idea" to getting upset with you, and none of it is a reflection of your value or whether you're on the right path.

A colleague of mine who is living her dream job of professional traveling said the hardest part of her journey was what she called the "non-support"—the number of people who put doubts in her head—or who said, "You're crazy; don't do this!" to her. When I asked what she does when those voices creep into her thoughts, she mentioned exactly what we've discussed in this chapter: have a community. There are many possible reasons for the naysayers' behavior that likely have nothing to do with you.

> "In life, there are people who will ultimately add to you, and people who will ultimately take away from you."
> — My dad

A clinical psychologist once told me that people in a long-term system (like a family) tend to assume roles—the scapegoat, the vocal one, the encourager, the devil's advocate, and so on—and that, as you begin changing, many will resist and speak out against you changing your "role." If this happens, remember that they may just be experiencing a normal human reaction to change. Be patient with them, keep moving, and focus on your supporters.

What should you do with your supporters and naysayers?

Allocate more of your time to your supporters and away from your naysayers

It doesn't mean that you have to cut anyone out of your life—just that you prioritize spending time with those who believe in you during this process. Why wait? Reach out to one of your supporters now and ask them what they appreciate about you or what qualities they think you have that will make you succeed. (Seriously—right now. If you're hesitant, just tell them that you're reading a book about career purpose and this is an exercise you're supposed to do.) Then, put their answers on your wall, or on stickies by your desk, or in another place that you'll see regularly. Read them every day to remind yourself of the truth.

Keep your list of supporters and their comments about you easily accessible for when you need a boost

If you've had a bad day, have forgotten your value, or need encouragement to keep going, these are your people to reach out to. Keeping the list close by makes it much easier and therefore more likely that you'll contact one of them. You can also keep digital or paper copies of their encouraging comments handy for an on-demand pick-me-up. I keep a digital note called "Encouragement" with screen captures of uplifting text messages or feedback from clients, and an email folder called "Happy Things," where I drag a copy of any email that makes me smile for a reminder later. The key, as the header suggests, is for these to be easily accessible at all times.

Intentionally grow your list of supporters

There are many ways you could do this; one is to ask the people on your list to introduce you to the people in *their* life who lift them up. Who are their mentors, supporters, encouragers? Your supporters will happily connect you to their supporters because they want you to succeed. Another way is to keep track of every time someone says, "Let me know how I can help," and make a note of how they offer to help you as you begin sharing about your career purpose journey. You never know when you'll need them! If you need more inspiration, you can find additional ways to get connected on our website at www.CareerPurposeBook.com.

Practice allowing the comments from the naysayers to pass by you

When you come across negative or difficult comments from your naysayers, give yourself permission to let the comments go. By *let go*, I don't mean "resist them" or "fight against them," which can actually make the situation worse as we'll discuss in chapter seven. Rather, I mean to recognize them as not being the truth about you. As Ruiz and Mills wisely said in *The Four Agreements: A Practical Guide to Personal Freedom*, "Nothing other people do is because of you. It is because of themselves." (Check out the second agreement in that book for an extended lesson on this subject.)[16]

You can care about someone *and* not like what they have to say or internalize their comments about you. This is not easy for everyone, but with practice, it becomes easier. Compassion meditation is a useful tool that you can practice; or, you can just try taking a deep breath, recognizing that they have their own battles,

> "Nothing other people do is because of you. It is because of themselves."
> — *Ruiz and Mills*, The Four Agreements

and moving forward. Then, reach out to one of your supporters to remind you that you're on the right path.

Note: If you're struggling with letting go of these types of comments from naysayers, it could be an important clue that limiting beliefs or fears may be at play. Their comments may be similar in wording to your limiting belief or fear, and therefore, hearing them say these things about you can trigger a disproportionate emotional response. We will cover strategies to help with these beliefs and fears in chapter seven, but for now, you may wish to explore whether this is something that you are experiencing through journaling, conversation with a loved one, or with a licensed professional.

If you have someone toxic in your life, prioritize working your way away from them

I sincerely hope that nobody reading this is frequently around a toxic individual. These types of people go well beyond telling you that your idea won't work; over time, they affect your mental health and risk making you believe the negative things that they say about you. If you have someone like this in your life, prioritize the transition away from them (with professional help, if needed) so that they will not keep pulling you down. You deserve better than to be held back by them in any way!

*   *   *

As you read through this foundation, which two to three supporters come to mind as those who you can begin allocating more of your time and energy toward today? There's no time like the present to get started; why not begin by setting up a time to chat with them before you continue to the next foundation?

FOUNDATION #3: FUEL YOURSELF FOR THE JOURNEY

To use a vehicle analogy, you need to fill your tank with fuel for the journey to find and live your career purpose. This step is especially important for those in a draining situation, who are feeling burned out, or are in constant "firefighting" mode—that is, those who are low on fuel or running on empty—because the work to find your career purpose is the kind that isn't as urgent unless you make it so. It is easy to put off, because it won't be hunting you down if you miss the time to work on it. However, the interesting dynamic that you'll notice from implementing this section is that adding these fueling activities to your week doesn't take away time from doing other things—it "adds" time! (You'll see what I mean shortly.) It doesn't matter whether you feel drained in your personal or in your professional life, either. Without fuel, you won't have the time or energy to dedicate yourself fully to either one. Let's review two research-backed strategies to ensure that you're equipped for the "road" ahead.

Strengths

In mid-April 2020, the COVID-19 pandemic was in full swing. At the time, I was incredibly blessed with a part-time job while I was building my facilitation and coaching business. I had the honor of working with a team of amazing people, all the flexibility that I needed to work remotely and build the business, and I was learning and growing every day. But the relevant part of this story is that, while I was great at the skills required for the job and had many wonderful colleagues and benefits, the work itself drained me. We all have activities that strengthen us—that we can't wait to do!—and activities that drain us. That's part of life, and in normal times, the balance was optimal. When the pandemic hit, though, all of my coaching and facilitation work came to a screeching halt as companies faced layoffs and sudden changes, putting talent development on the back burner amidst the crisis.

I then found myself struggling to find the energy and motivation to do my other work. While I made sure to still maintain a high-quality level of performance, doing so somehow took much more out of me than it used to. I was so drained that I called my career coach for advice on a strategy for transitioning to full-time business ownership; I had come to the incorrect conclusion that I needed to leave the part-time role. As any wise coach does, she wondered if we were talking about the "real" problem. She pushed back gently: "Ashley, I think we need to look at how to manage your energy levels instead."

I could have smacked myself.

"I TEACH THIS STUFF!" I gasped in disbelief. I couldn't believe that I had missed the point entirely—it wasn't that I needed to leave, it was that my "fuel tank" to complete this work was empty! This gave me the insight that I needed to know exactly what to do: I immediately texted a friend who had expressed interest in a coaching session with me and booked a call with her. I didn't even care about money at the time—I just needed to coach somebody, STAT! What fascinated me about this experience was that, after that coaching appointment and incorporating more of the activities that fueled me into my week, I was the same person, in the same part-time job, doing the same part-time work . . . but after adding coaching to my week, I had the fuel to do the work.

What are strengths?

I first heard Marcus Buckingham speak about the activities he calls "strengths" at a conference several years ago and have followed his work ever since. When it comes to the journey to find your career purpose, I consider his work on strengths to be a critical concept to apply. He defines a strength as *an activity that strengthens you*—not necessarily one that you are skilled at doing. "It draws you in," he says. "It makes time fly by while you're doing it, and it makes you feel strong." These activities are the ones you're doing when you look up and realize that it's been three hours, but it felt like ten minutes, and when you have to stop, you can't wait to do the activity again.[17]

> "You often feel tired, not because you've done too much, but because you've done too little of what sparks a light in you."
> — *Alexander Den Heijer,*
> Nothing You Don't Already Know

When I first heard about this concept, I thought of how much I enjoyed having one-on-one conversations in my office with various staff members where I worked. I loved hearing what they were interested in and how I could help them. I now realize that most of that was an early form of coaching—one of my strengths. It's an activity that strengthens me, makes me feel alive, and makes me feel like time flies by. For our purposes, your strengths could be any activity—personal or professional—that gives you this same feeling.

The reason it's important to allocate time to these strengthening activities (which I will hereafter refer to as "strengths," to align with Buckingham's terminology) into your week as we're applying them to your career purpose journey is that if you don't have fuel in your tank, or if the rate of refueling isn't faster than the rate at which you are burning fuel, then at some point, the vehicle will no longer run. Eventually, you will experience burnout—if you haven't already—and that's a truly difficult state in which to go on this journey. Conversely, if you incorporate the "right" amount of these strengths into your week, you will have the fuel to tackle it all.

What is the "right" amount of time to spend on strengths?

Buckingham also shared research from *Mayo Clinic Proceedings* about doctors experiencing burnout, and how much time they needed to spend on their strengths to prevent burnout from occurring. What percent of your week would you guess that you would need to spend on strengths in order to avoid burnout? When I ask this question, the average answer people give me is around 50 to 80 percent. Makes sense, right? Those activities we dislike are really draining. I have some good news, though: The number is only 20 percent! Twenty! This gives us so much hope. If you're in a job that drains you, you can easily find time for your strengths on nights and weekends to fuel you until you're able to make a change, or work with your team to tweak your role slightly, or help with some special projects at work. (We'll talk more about these ideas in chapter six.) However you choose to do it, that magical 20-percent, break-even point of your time allocated to strengths will be the fuel that you need to avoid burnout on the path to finding your career purpose.[18]

What about you? To identify your own strengths, ask yourself: what were you doing the last time that you felt truly alive, or felt like your best self? It could be any activity—reading, planning, encouraging others, analyzing data, engaging in intellectual discussion, solving complex problems, identifying efficiencies in your organization's processes, or whatever makes time pass lightning fast for you. Make sure to note a few initial ideas for now; we'll come back to these soon. If you're struggling to come up with ideas, Buckingham suggests living the process—that is, notice as you go about your week when you feel that sense of being truly alive, time flying by quickly, and a desire to do that activity again soon—and make a note of what activity you were doing at the time.[18]

Then, as Stephen R. Covey said in *The 7 Habits of Highly Effective People*, "The key is not to prioritize what's on your schedule, but to schedule your priorities." In this case, prioritize spending at least 20 percent of your week on your strengths before all the other, urgent to-dos of life creep into your schedule, and you'll have the fuel in your tank to complete the journey. Put strengths in your calendar *first*.[19]

If you're feeling overwhelmed at the idea of including anything else on your schedule, remember that, because these activities fuel you, it will feel more like *adding* time than taking it away. One of my coaching clients wasn't so sure about this. "I was skeptical at first," she admitted to me on one of our calls. "But when I carved out time on a Sunday afternoon for my strengths, I felt like I'd had a more leisurely Sunday than I've had in a long time (even though it was just an hour or two). Most importantly, I still had time to do all the other things. It was really nice, actually!"

Pause for a moment and add one or two of the strengths that you've identified into your calendar in the next couple of days to begin forming the habit of including them in your week.

Meditation

Hear me out if you're skeptical on this one, because I was too. I felt like I'd heard about meditation everywhere but didn't see how dedicating the time when I was already so busy would really benefit me. Those who told me I should try it sent me resources, ideas, documents, links—you name it. What finally clicked for me was a moment in an online workshop that I attended in which the facilitator shared with us that it would only take eight minutes per day to achieve benefit from the practice of meditation. "Eight!" I thought. "I can find eight minutes for a few days to try this." This inspired me to search for guided meditation videos online, which made the practice quite easy as I sat there and listened to the instructions from the guide.[20]

While the positive effects of mindfulness meditation—such as reduced stress, burnout, depression, and pain; and increased quality of life, sense of well-being and empathy (just to name a few!)—are already documented, those effects are not the main reasons that I included it here. The benefit relevant to our *career purpose* journey that I personally found to be true was the ability to better focus my attention on a single task at a time—even in the face of many distractions or things that would normally raise my stress levels—and therefore, more energy (fuel!) to use for longer hours. In short, I was more focused, present, energetic, and proactive on the journey. Given the volume of studies about the negative effects of multitasking and distraction on our performance and our minds, and the constant and ever-increasing information overload of today's world, we *need* the fuel and focus that meditation gives us for our career purpose journey.[21,22,23,24]

What about you? With such little time commitment, and readily available apps and videos to tell you exactly what to do, why not try it for yourself? Every day for one week, try eight to ten minutes of mindful meditation practice and see what changes you notice. If you're a novice, just add "beginner" to your search term. There is no "correct" time of day in which to engage in the practice, but I found it helpful to do in the middle of the day as a brain refresher, and also because I tended to doze off if I tried to do it in the morning or evening. See what works for you—go ahead and add this to your calendar, too, before you continue. Similar to the strengths from the last section, consistent meditation will not feel like adding extra time to your already-busy schedule; rather, it will unlock your ability to do more.

FOUNDATION #4: FOCUS ON THE POSSIBILITIES AND SUCCESS AHEAD

One day, my husband found me pacing around in the driveway talking to myself.

"Uh . . . what are you doing?" he asked, seemingly wondering if I'd lost my mind.

"I'm telling myself all the reasons my workshop is going to go well," I replied. I was about to deliver a workshop to a group of high-level leaders who had indicated potential interest in purchasing the same workshop for their direct reports, depending on how this one went. I knew there was much at stake, and I recognized that if I focused on what I stood to lose, I would be nervous in my delivery, and manifest the exact outcome I was afraid of—that I would screw it up.

"Well, I hope that works for you," he offered.

"You don't understand!" I protested. "There *is* no other possible outcome." I had been at this a while, and I had succeeded at convincing myself. "I *will* do an amazing job. They *will* love me and want to purchase more workshops after this one," I said with conviction.

"Okay then," he laughed, probably still convinced that I had lost my mind, but supportive of anything that would work for me. He went about his business, and I continued repeating these phrases to myself.

One Saturday a few weeks after the workshop, an email popped into my inbox. "Good news!" it said. My heart jumped. They wanted to buy more workshops—*five* more!

> "Our perceptions determine, to an incredibly large degree, what we are and are not capable of. In many ways, they determine reality itself."
> — *Ryan Holiday,*
> The Obstacle Is the Way

Research shows that if we have strong enough commitment and motivation levels for a specific plan of action, our unconscious mind takes over and operates automatically (that is, without a conscious intent) when the situation arises. If that sounds like a bunch of academic jargon, the point is that whatever you focus your thoughts on is the reality that you will manifest automatically when the time comes. It is no wonder that the practices of affirmations and visualization are so prevalent in books on success.[25,26]

Try it yourself: The next time you're concerned about how a certain situation, performance, conversation, or meeting will turn out, try focusing on the best possible outcome and all that you stand to gain (talking to yourself while pacing in the driveway is optional!). I have seen repeatedly in my own experience how my subsequent behaviors align on auto-pilot with my thoughts when I do this. Think of all the wonderful outcomes that you could manifest if you make this a practice on the journey to find your career purpose!

Another way in which we limit ourselves unnecessarily on this journey is by having "blinders" on and missing opportunities that present right in front of our face. What would happen if we were more open to the possibilities that life could bring us?

I once read about a research study that forever changed my mindset about success and luck. The study, conducted by Richard Wiseman, investigated why some people are lucky and others aren't. Wiseman gave a copy of a newspaper to people who self-identified as either exceptionally lucky or exceptionally unlucky. Their task was to report the number of photos that they could find within the newspaper. Those who considered themselves to be exceptionally lucky more frequently noticed a giant ad on the second page that informed them there were exactly forty-three photos, and thus they stopped counting, finishing the task much quicker than their counterparts. Those who considered themselves exceptionally *un*lucky seemed to miss this ad while focusing on the photo-counting task. For me, the next part is where the study gets especially interesting. Wiseman had placed a second giant ad later on in the newspaper, this time informing the participants that they could stop counting, tell him they saw the ad, and receive $250. Guess who saw this second, giant ad more often? You guessed it—the people who considered themselves to be exceptionally lucky.[27]

What about you? What do you make of this study? Is there really such a thing as luck? Do you think that I and others who are in their dream job are just the "lucky" few? I think this study gives us great freedom to know that we can *all* make our own "luck" if we are just open to the possibilities that may come our way. As you continue on the path to finding your career purpose, you can choose to keep an open mind and to be excited about what can and will come your way. You never know what ideas, people, resources, or whatever else might show up on your path, and it's incredibly unlikely that the path will look exactly as you picture it before you start. So, will you be ready for the unforeseen opportunities when they appear, or will you miss them entirely because you have "blinders" on? What positive potential outcomes could you focus your thoughts on more? What possibilities could be on their way to you, if you're just open to seeing them?

If you need a little more guidance on shifting your mindset, this is a great coaching or mentoring topic. A coach who understands a successful mindset, or a mentor who's found success in your chosen industry, can help shepherd you through the process of seeing how you're currently thinking and how to transform those thoughts to focus on what you want and all the exciting possibilities that await you.

You could also pay closer attention to your self-talk by noting your thoughts as you have them, and then observing any patterns. Do you tend to think more positive or more negative thoughts about your future? Do you focus more on what you stand to gain versus what you're afraid might happen? Do you have a balance of thoughts about today's to-dos *and* all the exciting things ahead for you?

Regardless of how you go about it, adopting a mindset in which you focus on the possibilities and successes that are coming your way, while also remaining grateful, content, and proud of your current situation, will help you in many more ways beyond finding your career purpose.

FOUNDATION #5: ADDRESS ANYTHING THAT YOU'VE BEEN AVOIDING

Successfully identifying and going after your career purpose is a journey that requires a whole mind, body, and spirit approach. I know—I drive a hard bargain, but I've seen over and over how this journey is something that you have to *fully* commit to doing. Because nobody can do it for you, you must do it relentlessly, no matter what it takes. If you go on the journey with unaddressed issues

> Successfully identifying and going after your career purpose is a journey that requires a whole mind, body, and spirit approach.

in your life, they can become like RAM in the "computer" of your mind, taking up background processing space and limiting your capacity to dedicate yourself to this mission—or worse, even derailing you from the mission. While you certainly don't have to wait until everything is perfect in your life to continue in this process, if you do not acknowledge and begin to address these items that are holding you back, you can simply expect to continue to be held back by them along this journey.

Let's say that you have a strained relationship with a colleague. Perhaps each time that you see them, you feel distracted or your mood might dip slightly. The statistics I found on the costs of avoiding difficult conversations when preparing to teach workshops on how to navigate them are truly sobering. Avoiding these conversations impacts not only our personal and professional relationships, but everything from organizational success, to manager productivity, to our mental and physical health. It's as if they're slowly eating away at our well-being, largely unbeknownst to us, while we avoid addressing them. The good news is that we can repurpose that mental energy toward the work on our journey, if we seek to address what we've been avoiding.[28]

Another example could be if you've become so busy at work that you've recently neglected any spiritual, religious, or community activities that you were previously doing in your free time. What made you do them in the past—was it a sense of calm, belonging, or perspective? What could you stand to gain if you picked these activities back up? Or perhaps there's something unresolved from your past—whether physical or emotional—nagging at you to come back to it and find healing or closure.

I'm not pretending any of this is easy to address, only pointing out the mental space it takes up when it continues to go unresolved, and the opportunity we have to free up our capacity for energy, resources, and well-being on this journey.

Lastly, I believe—and have found to be the case in my own experience—that opportunities come to you only when you're ready for them. That means our job is to prepare ourselves for all the exciting things coming to us, and working on these unaddressed items is a fantastic way to start.

What about you? Are there items in your life that you need to address—whether big or small? You'll know deep down if there's anything that you've been avoiding. I had a health coach once who would frequently ask me "What does your wise woman inside say?" Even if it wasn't something I wanted to hear, that darn "wise woman" always knew what I needed to do. What might the wise person inside you want to say if you were open to hearing it? Do you need to return to proper amounts of sleep, exercise, or nutrition? Seek therapy for an event in your past? Have a difficult conversation? Find someone who can help you with a physical injury that hasn't healed properly? Finally address your concerns about the amount of alcohol you or a loved one consumes? You deserve better than to settle for momentary inspiration or "that would be nice if . . ." kind of thinking. We all have challenges, so whatever you're dealing with is normal. While finding your career purpose won't "fix" something else going on in your life, the good news is that you don't have to solve any of these challenges today. Sometimes, just thinking of *one*, first step that you could take to make a positive change in your life and free up mental resources for your career purpose journey is all you need.

A QUICK RECAP

Now that we've reviewed how to build a solid foundation, have you addressed each of the areas in this chapter? If you haven't, don't let a lack of time stall your progress! Here is a quick recap that is framed as a high-level version that you can do in just a few minutes:

- Make a couple of positive updates to your current environment. Even something as simple as putting one item in its place or opening a window can help.
- Send a quick message to one of your supporters for a boost. If you can't think of anything to say, just thank them for supporting you.
- Book a time for your strengths (remember, these are activities that make you feel truly alive and time passes quickly while you do them) and mindfulness meditation in your calendar this week so that you have adequate fuel for the journey.
- Consider at least one exciting possibility coming your way soon. What would you love to see happen? What *could* happen for you if you're just open to seeing it?
- Identify one next step to address anything that you've been avoiding, no matter how small. Whether it's a matter of mind, body, or spirit, we all have something that we can improve to take a little "weight off our shoulders."

Finally, which of these components do you need to implement on a more detailed level in order to set yourself up for success and surround yourself with positivity on this journey? Are there any others that you should include that are not listed here?

*   *   *

You now have a sturdy foundation built to ensure your success along this path. Feel free to return to this chapter anytime that you need a refresher—it's important to keep your foundation strong as you move along the path.

Now, let's find out what your career purpose is!

Note: Some of the inspiration for this chapter and the ideal day exercise came in part from a book called *You're a Badass at Making Money* by Jen Sincero. By the time that I applied this inspiration to the career purpose journey and included stories, examples, and research studies, it became complex as to where to reference specific points. I would therefore like to give a broader acknowledgement to her book, and to express a sincere thanks for the profound effect it had on my ability to generate income in my dream job, enabling me to do it full-time. Looking back at the book, I noticed a small, serendipitous quote within it that I had previously missed: "[Y]ou can figure out how to flourish doing what you love." My hope is that my book serves as a methodology for doing so, and if you also want to learn how to manifest a robust income doing what you love, please do yourself a favor and read her book.[29]

PART II

FINDING YOUR CAREER PURPOSE

CHAPTER 3
FOLLOW YOUR LEADS . . . RELENTLESSLY

"The meaning of life is to find your gift.
The purpose of life is to give it away."
— *Pablo Picasso*

In chapter one, I shared a story of how I followed a series of clues, or leads, based on how I felt along my path to find my career purpose. You may recall that I mentioned an inner "feelings compass" that guided me from lead to lead on that path; it was only when I started following it that I began heading in the right direction. This chapter is all about how to tune in to, and follow, that compass to find and explore your own leads. The process described here is the core, lifelong strategy to find and live your career purpose, one that will need to become a habit to successfully navigate the journey. That's why I have given it its own chapter before we review the other components of your career purpose—it is the heart of this book.

FIRST THINGS FIRST: IF YOU WANT TO KNOW YOUR CAREER PURPOSE, YOU HAVE TO GET COMFORTABLE WITH FEELINGS

Gasp! I know—feelings! They can have such a negative reputation some-times, but the truth is that the path to finding your career purpose is not a logical one—it's primarily an emotional one.

> The path to finding your career purpose is not a logical one – it's primarily an emotional one.

Let that sink in for a moment. To find your career purpose, you must go *beyond* the logical and the rational.

To be clear, I'm not suggesting that you become overly emotional or talk openly everywhere about your feel-ings. I simply mean that, to find your career purpose, you must intention-ally notice how ideas make you *feel* as you encounter them, and then follow the ones that create the more exciting feelings while moving away from the ones that create the more repulsive feelings.

In case you're skeptical, this strategy isn't about discounting logic or reason. In his book *The Body Keeps the Score*, psychologist Dr. Bessel van der Kolk contends that "[E]motion is not opposed to reason; our emotions assign value to experiences and thus are the foundation of reason." Taking a closer look at this strategy, we find that it is an investigation or experiment that is quite scientific in nature. You are the researcher, and what you feel in your body when you encounter various ideas related to work—such as read-ing a job description, hearing someone talking about their job, or consider-ing an idea for a potential career path—is the most direct *data point* that I have found for identifying your career purpose.[30]

To explore why this is, I conducted a search for articles about neurosci-ence, logic, emotion, and purpose. I'll spare you the details of the "rabbit hole" that I went down, looking into pathways, regions, and processes of the brain. (You're welcome!) The two most helpful pieces of information I found were: that two different parts of the brain govern logic and emotion, and that they are extremely effective when coordinated well. It seems to me, therefore, that if what you're looking for is fulfillment (a *feeling*), then you must tap into the parts of your brain associated with emotion, not just the ones associated with logic and reasoning. This chapter describes how to do so.[31]

Does this mean that we should throw out the logical and rational approaches? Heavens, no! The standard approach to seeking your next job or career provides important, practical insights, and it should in no way be disregarded. However, if we're looking for meaningful and fulfilling work, the standard approach should be used *in addition to* the feeling-based one described in this chapter. A career coach, career transition program or book, or the wealth of information online will help you enhance your résumé with your past work experience, tailor your cover letter to job descriptions, learn how to answer behavioral interview questions using the STAR (Situation, Task, Action, and Result) method, practice presenting how your experience and skills are a great match for the hiring organization, negotiate a salary, and so on. If you are not already familiar with these steps, please seek assistance with them as part of your career purpose journey; we will not cover them in this book since resources on them are readily available. The other reason that we won't cover the standard process is that it does not primarily focus on helping you find work that *feels* purposeful and meaningful.

This focus brings us to a critical point: *To get to a feeling-based endpoint (fulfillment), you have to use a feeling-based process.* Further, because nobody else can feel what you feel, nobody else can do this work for you.

> To get to a feeling-based endpoint, you have to use a feeling-based process.

To illustrate what I mean, think about the last time that you read a job description, or heard somebody talking about what they do for a living. (If you can't think of a specific example, pause and do a quick search so you can read a job description—any one of them will do—before you continue.)

As you read or heard the details, did you feel a sense of excitement bubbling up? A sense of how fun it sounds? Or did you feel a sense of repulsion—perhaps you cringed at parts of it, thinking something like "Wow, I'm really glad that's not my job!"

These are the kinds of feelings that I'm talking about following when I say that you have to follow a feeling-based process. As you can probably imagine, this part of the career-searching process tends to go largely unleveraged. If you want to find your career purpose, and not just the logical next step in your current career trajectory, these feelings need to come off the "back burner" to the forefront of your mind and be your primary guide.

You could be amazing at—and have decades of experience in—a job you dislike or that drains you. It could have all the perks in the world, a high salary, and great colleagues, but if you come home at the end of the day feeling drained, empty, stressed, or burned out, then none of the skills, experience, or perks will give you a sense of fulfillment. Unfortunately, that means that if you exclusively follow a logical, predictable career path from an unfulfilling role to find your next role, you risk getting more of that which is unfulfilling to you. As Daniel Goleman wrote in *Emotional Intelligence: Why It Can Matter More than IQ*, "The key to sounder personal decision-making, in short: being attuned to our feelings."[32]

WHAT ARE EMOTIONAL LEADS?

I refer to these feelings that you experience when encountering various ideas about work—and that you must follow in order to find your career purpose—as "emotional leads." Whatever your opinion about a process of following your feelings is at this point, the bottom line is that *the key to finding your career purpose is to identify and follow these emotional leads, and to do it relentlessly.* They may be small and hard to notice—like a small spark or a slight discomfort—or they may make you feel like "jumping out of your body" or screaming. The stronger the positive feeling, the closer you are to your career purpose. The stronger the negative feeling, the further you are from your career purpose.

> The key to finding your career purpose is to identify and follow your "emotional leads," and to do it relentlessly.

As you continue to follow your emotional leads (which I will refer to hereafter as "leads" for the sake of being concise) the feeling that you feel will get stronger, just as a metal detector begins beeping more rapidly as it gets closer to a metal object. And, just as you would experience if you were searching for metal in the sand at a beach, the metal isn't going to come looking for you. You must proactively go searching for it yourself. Because nobody else can do this work for you, and because we all have seemingly endless distractions vying for our attention at all times, you must follow your leads *relentlessly.*

*   *   *

One afternoon early in my career purpose journey, I made a drive across Atlanta to meet with a mentor at a coffee shop. After placing our orders, we sat down by the window in some comfy chairs, taking in the aroma of fresh coffee as the sound of conversations and the espresso machine buzzed in the background. During the course of our conversation, he told me about a project that he was working on that would train new managers in leadership skills. At the time, I had not yet identified my career purpose, and I will never forget how I felt when he asked a question that gave me the strongest lead that I've ever had: "Ashley, would you like to be a coach for new managers?"

My heart nearly jumped out of my chest! I have never felt such a strong desire to scream, cry, and jump up and down—all at once. I reigned it in so as not to cause a scene, and I chuckle now as I remember him commenting that he wasn't sure how to read my expression. (Can you imagine the look on my face trying to hold all that in? Hilarious.) I didn't know it at the time, but what I was feeling was my strongest lead yet—leadership training and coaching, particularly for early-career professionals—and all I had to do was continue down that path to see where it led more specifically.

HOW DO YOU FIND A LEAD?

Consider the following questions to help you generate an initial list of lead ideas. You may wish to note them down in a journal or discuss with a loved one:

What are you particularly curious about or drawn to?

Your lead could be in any form: a certain industry or role, the way somebody completes a task, a certain person who has professional skills that you admire, a workplace culture, or any aspect of work. Ask yourself: Have you noticed some aspect of a job—any job—that piqued your curiosity? What about it seems to draw you in? What is there to further explore?

Let's say that you were invited to help plan an orientation for new students and felt drawn to it for some reason. You could explore whether you're drawn to an event-planning role, or the hospitality industry in general, or the project management tool that the team used to organize each task, or how you encouraged a nervous new student who wasn't sure where to go. Or maybe you have a friend who seems particularly happy in their role and you're curious about why, or you have always thought a particular role or industry seemed intriguing but never really looked much into it. Now is the time to explore these thoughts.

What do you avoid doing or procrastinate about?

This feeling gives you valuable information about what your purpose is *not*. It doesn't matter how good you are at the task, how much you think you *should* be doing that task in your career, how long you've been doing it, or how many people tell you that you should do it (or tell you that you can't stop because you're too good at it!). The only clue to pay attention to here is if you feel a sense of resistance or repulsion away from it. The stronger the sense of repulsion, tightness in your chest, or other negative feeling, the stronger the indication that you're moving away from your career purpose. These moments can feel like your inner compass screaming, "Run far away!" Ask yourself what it is specifically about that task, environment, method, culture, tool—or whatever it is—that is so *un*attractive to you?

What kind of work sounds exciting or fun to you?

Have you ever had a moment like the one that I described above with my mentor in the coffee shop, where I heard about a potential line of work that sounded amazing? The stronger the positive emotion that you felt, the stronger the lead is, and therefore, the more direct the correlation to your career purpose. Perhaps you haven't had a moment that strong, but you may notice as you go about your day that some ideas seem more exciting than others. Just noticing a lead is a huge first step. Ask yourself: what kind of work seems the most fun or exciting to you and makes you want to dive deeper? You might write off the idea of doing this type of work as a career, thinking that it's unlikely you could make a living doing something *that* fun. We can sometimes turn them into hobbies that we do for free, missing the opportunity to make a living at them if we had just given it more thought and effort. Have you ever had the thought, "You mean I could get *paid* to do that?" That's the kind of work I'm talking about here.

What tasks do you know you enjoy doing?

Make a list of tasks that you already know you enjoy, regardless of whether they are currently part of your personal or professional life. Your strengths that you identified in chapter two are a great start! Ask yourself what kinds of tasks you wish that you could do, all day every day, in a perfect world—or which parts of your current job you enjoy the *most*. Many of my coaching clients say that they know the answer to this question but have navigated away from those tasks in lieu of others that they think are more practical. Now is the time to call them back to the forefront of your mind and consider them in your list of possible leads.

We'll discuss more about how strengths and leads overlap in the next chapter, but if you could use some clarification at this point on how they are different (since both are found through the feelings that they give you), remember that strengths are specific activities that *strengthen*—or, as we are applying them, *fuel* you—for the journey. The leads that I'm talking about in this chapter are the clues from your "inner compass," indicating whether you're moving toward or away from your career purpose. Leads could be in many forms: a process, an environment, a company, a culture, a cause, a degree—to name a few—whereas strengths are exclusively activities.

More specifically, by Buckingham's definition, strengths are activities that you look forward to doing, feel "flow" during, and fulfillment afterward. It therefore seems to me that you'd need to experience them directly to know whether they are a strength, whereas you can find leads anywhere—through conversations, observation, reading about them, or seeing them in movies, without having directly experienced them. While a strength can certainly also be a lead—as in my case with coaching and teaching—a lead is not always a strength by Buckingham's definition, nor are we applying these ideas with the same context or purpose. For further reading and research on what strengths are and the critical role that they play in both individual and team performance, check out Lie #4 in the book *Nine Lies About Work: A Freethinking Leader's Guide to the Real World* co-authored by Buckingham and Goodall.[33]

It is not necessary for you to be an expert on the terminology to keep moving through this process; for now, just focus on what kinds of tasks that you already know you enjoy doing to consider as potential leads.

Have you ignored any "I just knew" moments?

Many of us have had an experience at some point in our lives in which we saw someone doing a particular job, or watched a television show or movie about it, or read a book about it, and something ignited inside us. We "just knew" in that moment that's what we were meant to do. I've met several people (and seen many more interviewed) who have had this kind of experience, but then wrote off the emotion with any number of logical reasons why they couldn't go after that career.

Have you had any moments like this? Maybe you saw a magician perform when you were a child and instantly knew that's what you wanted to do when you grew up, but you convinced yourself that the chances of "making it" would be skewed against you and not worth the risk. Perhaps you have always known that you wanted to work in a public school system, or be a hairstylist, or a writer, but your family tried to convince you that you should be a doctor or lawyer like everyone else in the family. Maybe you knew the first time that you saw a rocket launch that you wanted to be an astronaut, or the first time you watched a certain sports game you longed to be on the field among the players—but you decided that you didn't have what it takes to do the amount of practice required or that it was too far-fetched to be your career choice.

The professional traveler whom I mentioned in the last chapter shared about a time in her childhood when she was watching a television show about a club of people who had traveled to over 100 countries. As she was watching the show with her parents, she turned to them and proclaimed: "That's going to me someday." How could she be so sure of this as a child? As an adult, wouldn't it be so easy to explain away all the reasons that she couldn't (or shouldn't) turn traveling into a paid job—or worse still, to listen to the naysayers who warned her repeatedly not to quit her job and to stay in her "stable career" in human resources? I'm happy to report that, today, she is thriving as a professional traveler for a living. If she can do it, why can't you?

Are there any moments in your life where you can recall feeling at the time that you knew what you were meant to do? What did you dream of doing as a child, or while you were in school? Or, on a simpler level, have you felt drawn to a particular profession, industry, or company, but just didn't pursue it for whatever reason? What have you told yourself about those moments—did you give logical reasons why you "couldn't" pursue them? What would you now say that those moments were trying to show you? If money and fear were no object, what career would you want to explore?

SO, YOU HAVE SOME LEADS. NOW WHAT?

Follow your leads

As you begin noticing what your leads are (based on how they make you feel), the next step is to follow the positive ones, seeking stronger and stronger ones by narrowing the focus. Once you identify any lead, no matter how strong or weak it feels, start doing more activities (or having more conversations, or doing more research, or reading more job descriptions, or watching more videos . . .) in this area based on whatever you *do* know that you like, and information will become clearer as you go.

There isn't a right or wrong way to go about following leads; it's more about trial and error. As soon as you find anything that you think is a lead, the idea is to put your "investigator hat" on and search for more clues along that same line. Keep following the feeling until it gets stronger or weaker, which tells you if you're going in the correct or wrong direction, respectively.

For example, let's say you feel a sense of excitement at the idea of working with numbers. To follow that lead, you could talk to a friend who works in accounting about what they do, look up a video about finance, or browse job descriptions in the field of data science—the possibilities are endless. Then let's say that, as you're watching the video about finance, your interest piques at one point when they're talking about the stock market. That means something about the stock market is your next lead, so you could then look for a list of local classes or read a book about investing and see what excites or repels you about those . . . and so on.

> Keep refining your search in the direction of the leads that give you the strongest positive feelings, getting more targeted and specific as you follow them.

It's important to note here that if a particular idea gives you no feelings one way or another, then it's not a lead. We don't have emotional reactions to everything. The key here is to *keep refining your search in the direction of the leads that give you the strongest positive feelings* (and away from the ones that give you negative feelings), *getting more targeted and specific as you follow them.*

Process your leads

Since this is a personal journey, there isn't a "one-size-fits-all" way to process the leads that you find. The key is to know yourself and how you work. I happen to be a low-structure type of person, so I have a very low-structure approach to this. If you like more structure, you may wish to keep a spreadsheet categorized by industry, role, organization, environment, etc. If you're introverted, you might want to capture them in a journal and process your thoughts and feelings by reflection. If you're extraverted, you might want to talk out the ideas with a loved one and get their input. If you like to make it up as you go, then you may want to just keep mental notes of the top two or three strongest emotions that you've felt through the process. Most importantly, you must be proactive in following your leads (relentlessly!), since it's much easier to slip back into our daily habits and react to the to-dos that come our way than it is to keep noticing and following our leads.

KEYS TO A SUCCESSFUL LEAD-FOLLOWING PROCESS

Keep other people's "clutter" out of your process

Nobody else is in your mind, and nobody else can feel how you feel. That means that other people's advice and opinions run a high risk of cluttering your lead-following process. (The exception is if one of your supporters or a coach is willing to guide you through processing and thinking through the information for yourself, as opposed to injecting their ideas and advice.)

Here's an example. When I first launched my business, I knew that I wanted to get a certification of some kind beyond my degree, for added credibility. I made the decision to become certified in a personality assessment as a tool to use with my coaching clients. The first lead came easily to me—my husband and I had long been intrigued by the Myers-Briggs Type Indicator® (MBTI®), often discussing it at the dinner table. Naturally, I thought that I should get certified in that assessment. As I began sharing this idea with colleagues, mentors, and friends, their opinions started creating doubts in me with all the logical reasons why I should become certified in a different assessment. The hardest part was that some of their logical arguments were tempting to follow, as they were soundly reasoned. Other assessments, they argued, might be easier for the audience to understand, or cost less for the reports, or be more prevalently used in a particular context, and so on. While I was tempted to change my approach, I decided to follow my lead—the feeling of excitement that I felt when I thought about getting certified in MBTI®. Conversely, when I thought about the other assessments they recommended, I just felt a flat feeling of general disinterest.

Boy, am I glad I listened to that lead. It's not to say that any one assessment is better than others; rather, that for me personally, this one was the one I could get excited about for my clients. Which one would you rather attend: a workshop with a facilitator who has a "flat" demeanor, or one who is excited about the topic? I don't know anybody who would choose the former. To this day, I have so much fun facilitating those workshops, and the participants feel it too. It gives me a sense of fulfillment and meaning to use this tool to help people better understand themselves and their colleagues, and if you practice following your leads, you can experience this feeling as well.

Just to be clear, I am not advocating keeping all of your decisions to yourself, or frivolously making completely feeling-based decisions, particularly when the decisions carry a cost. But think about the story that I just told from a financial perspective: Let's say I got certified in another assessment that my colleagues told me would be easier to sell. Even if the advice were correct in terms of raw numbers of clients who typically purchase the assessment, when I facilitated a workshop on it, the participants would be able to feel my lack of excitement and might therefore be less likely to purchase more workshops. However, because I followed my lead, the workshops naturally sell themselves, since I get excited talking about them (without even trying to sell anything), and people can feel that energy. In the longer run, which one do you think has been the better financial decision *in addition to* helping me live my career purpose?

While I encourage you to consider multiple angles and make the most responsible decision that you can, my point is to put more emphasis on (and trust in) your feelings about opportunities than in the advice of others *if* what you're looking for is the feeling of fulfillment in your work.

Don't let excuses stop you from following your leads

Now that you've made a commitment to find your career purpose and follow your leads, you can no longer engage in the "Yeah, but . . ." type of thinking. Let's say during this chapter, you've identified that painting is one of your leads. Sometimes, what happens next is that you catch yourself thinking an excuse about why you can't or shouldn't follow that lead, such as "Yeah, but I could never make money doing that." Remember: No excuses!

> "Excuses don't make things better; they are a way to rationalize to avoid trying."
> — Simon Sinek

One organization that I worked for paid $18,000 USD for *one* portrait of a retiring chairman. One. (That would be the equivalent of over $21,700 at the time this book was written, accounting for inflation.)

You *can* find a way to make a living doing what you love if you are willing to put in the effort. (See my note at the end of chapter two if you want a recommendation for a great book on how to do so.) As we saw earlier, the excuses that we tend to give for not going after our dreams—or for not going after the leads that direct us there—are often just stories that we've told ourselves to rationalize avoiding a deeper fear or limiting belief.

Note: I acknowledge that the term excuse *could have an unintended connotation; I am choosing the word to inspire action, not in any way to reprimand anyone for not having done so. You deserve more!*

How do you know if you're making an excuse?

Here are a few examples of common excuses that people have given me for why they can't go after their career purpose. As you read through them, consider whether you've said or thought something similar:

> It's too late for me (or I'm too old).
>
> I don't have what it takes to do that job.
>
> I can't afford the time or money for the degree, certification,
>   or licensing that I'd need.
>
> I need to wait until my kids are grown to pursue my passion.
>
> I don't have any passions or career aspirations.
>
> The work that I want to do is too hard to break into or would take
>   too long to make it happen.
>
> I'm actually happy in my job or grateful for it. (Yet you complain
>   about it every day.)
>
> I'm too far down this other career path to start over, particularly
>   with a pay cut.
>
> I'm too young or just starting out in my career.
>
> I'm retired! That "ship" sailed; my career is over.
>
> I lack the knowledge, tools, resources, or support that I need.
>
> I can't make money doing what I love.
>
> I don't know how or where to start.
>
> I don't have the skills, experience, credibility, or training that
>   I'd need to do that job.

Which of these examples resonate most with you? Using your own words, what might you have been telling yourself along these similar lines?

Notice these are all reasons why you "can't" or "shouldn't" do what you love.

... But what if you could? Are all of these reasons *definitely* true, with no possible way to ever get around them? Very unlikely.

How are excuses different than limiting beliefs?

You may notice at this point as you start uncovering any excuses that you've been making that they might look similar to the language of your limiting beliefs and fears from chapter one. However, they are not necessarily the same. For our purposes, excuses are the reasons or rationalizations that you give to *avoid* your limiting beliefs and fears (whether you do so consciously or not).

For example, if one of your limiting beliefs is that you're not allowed to ask for help or have your needs met, you might make the excuse that you're too busy to look for people in your network who could help. Or, if you have a fear of risk, you may find yourself giving people every possible excuse under the sun why you "can't" leave your job.

These excuses are often hard to spot because we are masterful at finding very legitimate, logical reasons to avoid our fears (and as such, I want to be clear that I am in no way making light of any difficult situations). This means that only *you* can identify whether, deep down, there is something else going on. If so, it's a normal part of being human, and we will work through these beliefs and fears in chapter seven.

> The possibilities are only as limited as you allow them to be, and you deserve a life of meaningful work.

For now, let's simply call out our excuses for what they are. If someone else can have their dream job, so can you. There's nothing that's more special or more unique about other people than you. The possibilities are only as limited as you allow them to be, and you deserve a life of meaningful work.

How to move past excuses

Sometimes, simply bringing your excuses to light is enough; my coaching clients often tell me that just the act of saying them out loud helps them realize how untrue or even silly they can be.

If you need more help to get beyond your excuses, try adding one magical, little word to them: *how*. If your excuse is, "I can't make money doing work that I love," then ask yourself: "*How* can I make money doing the work that I love?" or "How can I have *both* the work that I love *and* make an income doing it?" In fact, don't stop at just one answer; try generating a list of twenty to thirty possible ways. Or try thinking of ways that you could make ten times more income than what you think you need. (If you get stuck, consider what you might suggest to a friend if they were in your situation, or brainstorm ideas with one of your supporters.) These are great hacks to stretch your brain to come up with new options that might not have occurred to you previously. It's no longer an excuse to say that you "can't."

Another strategy that you can try is to test the assumptions you're making. Ask yourself questions like: Is it *really* true that [insert excuse]? Am I *really* too old, young, inexperienced, etc., or is there a deeper fear or limiting belief here? Can I *really* not do it, or could I learn how? Is it *really* impossible, or could I break it into smaller steps?

For example, if you always wanted to be a tour bus driver, but are not physically capable of lifting the luggage required to apply for the job due to your smaller stature, ask yourself: Are you sure? Some people might have the option of doing strength training and become capable of heavier lifting. Next, ask yourself what it is that you *really* love deep down about this prospect and what other similar, meaningful work could you do. Is there a way that you could do the work that you love, just in a different way? In the tour bus driver example, if it's not the heavy lifting that you love, but perhaps the interaction with people, could you find or create a job in which you are giving the verbal guided tour while someone else is doing the driving and lifting? Could you orient your schedule or environment to make the work that you want to do easier on any physical, mental, logistical, or other type of limitation you may have? No matter what you're going through, you can find a way to do meaningful work. It may be through a different schedule, format, or role than you initially envision; the first step is simply to ask yourself *how* you can do it.

> You DO have everything that you need, and you CAN have your dream job. Period!

There will always be a rationalization available to you for why you should not go after your dreams. Please, don't settle for living vicariously through me and others who are in their dream job! Do not allow these excuses to creep into your lead-following process and stall you on your path. Let's put them in their place and reveal the truth: You DO have everything that you need, and you CAN have your dream job. Period!

Turn "dead-end" leads or perceived failures into data points

At one point in my career, I was ready to give up. I was exhausted, overworked, and had no work-life balance. I had been searching for jobs in a particular industry for over a year but had nothing to show for it. I'd received a few interviews along the way with ultimately no success, and I was at a breaking point. I considered quitting without having another job lined up, because I felt like I couldn't continue for another day. Feeling deflated, I did what any good daughter would do in that moment—I asked my mom what she thought. She mentioned a new role that had come her way through word of mouth.

"Wouldn't this job be better than no job?" she suggested.

She had a point—besides, what did I have to lose? I contacted the hiring manager and happened to be exactly what they were looking for. Grateful for the growth opportunity, I accepted the position. However, the role and function that I'd tried with all my might for a year to get was gone from my grasp. I was at what felt like a dead end with my leads. I had "failed" to manifest my dream job. I fought this change of direction mentally for about six months afterward, wondering if I should try to leverage this role to stay on that original path somehow.

It turns out that fate had different plans for me. My perceived "failure" to find the kind of job that I thought I wanted landed me at the proverbial front doorstep of my career purpose! Not getting the type of role that I thought I wanted was arguably one of the best things that ever happened to me—the new path provided *much* more potent leads than the other one had.

> Not getting the type of role that I thought I wanted was arguably one of the best things that ever happened to me.

Here's an analogy to help illustrate my point: Sometimes, it can seem like a clinical trial "fails." A researcher develops a promising hypothesis, may go through a long process of application (and sometimes re-application) for funding, obtains a grant, recruits dozens—if not hundreds or thousands—of volunteers, spends years of effort, administration, analysis, money, and so on. And then, the answer emerges:

The hypothesis was wrong; the intervention did not work. But did the trial really "fail?" Or did it provide valuable, validated information to the scientific and medical communities?

As Thomas Edison famously said, "I didn't fail. I just found 10,000 ways not to make a lightbulb; I only needed to find one way to make it work."[34]

As you continue following your leads, the path to your career purpose will include information both about what *is* and what *is not* your career purpose. You have the power to choose to see the latter as just that—information— and allow these data points to guide you away from what *isn't* your career purpose, and toward what *is* your career purpose.

LIVING THE PROCESS

The strategy of following your leads as discussed in this chapter is a process you must *live*, both now and after you're in your dream job. If tuning into how you feel isn't something that you're naturally inclined to do, making it more of a habit will help guarantee that you continue to live a life of meaningful and fulfilling work. It may help to proactively set aside some time on a regular basis to reflect on the leads you feel most drawn to and to continually ask yourself the questions presented here.

I could end this book here by encouraging you to follow your leads since that is the core, most important strategy, but it takes *time* to live the process. Sometimes, it can even take years—seven, in my case!—so, what can you do after making your initial list of leads that we discussed here?

In the next chapter of our journey, we'll gather and clarify some of the other components of your career purpose that you can identify *today,* and we'll talk about how your leads fit into the bigger picture. As you put these components together, a picture of your career purpose will emerge, which we will then refine and clarify into your dream job(s). Ready to dive in?

CHAPTER 4
GATHER THE COMPONENTS OF YOUR CAREER PURPOSE

"The two most important days in your life are the day
you were born and the day you find out why."
— Mark Twain

One Saturday morning, your family is cleaning out a section of the closet with all the board games that you've collected over the years. (Sounds fun, huh?) You're given an old jigsaw puzzle and look down at it in your hands. It's not even in a box; that went missing years ago. The pieces are now scrambled together in a plastic baggie. Since it hasn't been put together in such a long time, nobody remembers what the image on the puzzle is, or whether all the pieces are there. Your task is to put together the puzzle to see what the image is, and to sort out which pieces do and do not belong. It will take some time, but the task is doable.

You empty the contents of the bag onto a nearby table, put on some music, and begin working. As you start inventorying and assembling the pieces, you realize that, over the years, some pieces went missing, others that don't seem to belong to this puzzle have been added to it, and some of the pieces that were there faded or lost the picture imprinted on them. Slowly, you piece it together with the help of others, and the image begins to take shape. As it becomes clearer, you can tell which pieces clearly don't belong and which ones are missing. You notice patterns in the colors and the shapes, and it becomes easier to put it together as you go. You locate the missing pieces in some of the other boxes. Finally, the pieces come together, and a beautiful image emerges.

∗   ∗   ∗

In this chapter, we will follow a similar inventorying exercise to collect the pieces of your career purpose "puzzle," and in the next chapter, we'll put the pieces that belong together into one or more dream jobs. That means that not all of the pieces that you collect in this chapter will fit into the puzzle (some might be hobbies or side projects), and you might have to get outside help to find others that are missing.

I encourage you to think of this chapter like a whiteboarding or brainstorming exercise where we are just collecting all the pieces into one place for now and saving the narrowing-down part for later. I would recommend that you use your favorite paper or digital note-keeping mechanism to collect all the pieces; or, if you want something more visual, you could use a literal whiteboard, flip chart paper, or sticky notes—do whatever is most fun and interesting to you! In the next chapter, we'll synthesize them together onto a single page from which your beautiful puzzle image will emerge.

Before we begin, I'll note that the goal of this chapter is to make the relatively abstract concept of career purpose more concrete, practical, and accessible for you. It is not necessarily meant to be an exhaustive or one-size-fits-all list of the components that go into your unique career purpose. Feel free to add or change parts if they come to mind as you go. As one of my coaching clients shared with me, perhaps the most powerful and liberating part of this process is that you are in 100 percent control of doing it in a way that best serves *you*. This is *your* puzzle, *your* life, *your* story, and *your* career purpose.

COMPONENT #1: DRAFT A CAREER PURPOSE STATEMENT

There's something truly powerful about putting specific words to your career purpose, even if you already have a sense of what it is in your mind. My clients often tell me that, once it's written down, they have a more concrete sense of a reality that they can no longer ignore. How you go about drafting it, or whether the draft has the perfect words, are less important than whether it gives you a clearer sense of direction. No matter where you are on this journey, you'll need a "North Star" to remind you where you're going and what truly matters.

You may recall that I defined a career purpose in chapter one as the way in which you go about accomplishing your life purpose (or mission) through the work that you do. This section is your opportunity to put specific words to those ideas, by combining both halves—namely, your life purpose plus the practical way in which you make income carrying out that purpose—into one statement. (We'll discuss how to reframe the "income" part if that doesn't happen to be a key factor for you.)

The reason both halves are important is that if you know your life purpose but don't have a sense of direction for how to make a living at it, the risk is that you won't fulfill that purpose because of how intimately our income is connected in our minds with survival. In other words, when given the option between fulfilling work that doesn't pay the bills, or draining work that *does* pay the bills, guess which one people understandably tend to choose.

As we discussed, I don't believe that we have two purposes—one for work and one for our lives; rather, I believe that there is a deeper, emotional half and a more practical half to your career purpose.

You can think of the career purpose statement that we'll draft in this section like a summary of your career purpose. You could say to a friend, "My career purpose is [insert statement]," and that would be accurate and brief enough to be appropriate for that context; but by itself, one statement is unlikely to give us enough practical or detailed information to identify a dream job that you can then go after. So, for our purposes, this statement will serve as the core component of your career purpose, upon which the rest of the components will be added for a clearer and more holistic view.

> You can think of your career purpose statement like a summary of your career purpose.

The first half: your life purpose

Because there are countless resources available for how to draft a personal mission or life purpose statement, I'll simply suggest a few ways that I've found helpful that you can try. In this first half, we're looking broadly to answer the big questions of life such as "Why you are here on this earth?"; "What matters most to you?"; and "What do you hope to leave as your legacy?" The goal is not to get "the" perfect purpose written down right away (what a daunting task!) but rather a draft from which you can gain direction and act accordingly. Here are a few ways to identify a life purpose that I've found to be helpful:

1. *Reflect on how you can help others based on the highest and lowest moments of your life.*

   I know—this is deep stuff, but some of the most fulfilling work you'll ever do is because of these intense moments. Take a couple of deep breaths and think back over the course of your life to a time when you had one of your greatest joys or worst pains. In what ways could you give that joy to others or prevent others from feeling that pain? For example, if a loved one passed due to cancer that could have been better mitigated through regular screenings or by living a healthier lifestyle, might your purpose be to enable greater awareness of or opportunities for health and wellness for others? What about a time when a loved one changed your life by believing in you—could your purpose be to invest in people in a similar way?

2. *Identify your core values.*

   Your values provide insight into what is most important to you in life and serve as the guiding principles by which you live and make decisions. Because they are so core to who you are, they also provide important clues into your life purpose. Some examples of values include: integrity, excellence, respect, open communication, candor, trust, love, and humor. If you do a search for "list of values" online, you'll find hundreds more to choose from; I would recommend narrowing down to no more than about three for this exercise. That doesn't mean you don't value the words that don't make the cut, just that we want the few *most* important ones for this activity.

   When it comes to how your values connect to your life purpose, here are a few examples to get you thinking. Let's say the single most important value to you is adventure; then, your life purpose may be finding the adventure in every moment and situation. Or, if you value joy, you may find great meaning in helping others celebrate life's wins, no matter how big or small. If you value directness, your purpose may involve being the one person in someone's life who has the courage to "tell them like it is." Perhaps you value innovation, in which case your purpose could be to bring out the ideas from the inner inventor in all of us, whether we think we have one or not.

3. *Look through examples of life purpose statements and see what resonates.*
   Sometimes, having a few examples to react to is all you need. You can find endless examples in an online search for "life purpose statement examples," but here is a sampling to get you started:

   > Simplify life's most difficult questions and moments to inspire action.
   > Empower people to share their truth with the world.
   > Protect the lives around me so that they feel safe taking risks.
   > Create environments where we can live in harmony with one another.
   > Inspire people to leave the legacy of their mark on the world.
   > Provide a source of hope to everyone I meet.
   > Be a listening ear so that people can feel truly heard.
   > Shine a light on the beauty in every person's story.

   As you look through these examples, what stands out to you about them, and which parts could you apply (in your own words) to *your* life mission or purpose? Try to be as specific as possible with your draft; generic statements are perfectly fine as a starting point, but in order to gain a sense of direction, you'll need to go deeper as you refine your draft.

4. *Draft a WHY statement through Simon Sinek's WHY discovery process.*
   Out of all the methods that I've encountered for putting words to one's life purpose, this is the one that I found to be the most helpful and impactful. The process will yield a phrase in the form of "to [contribution] so that [impact]."[35]
   Some examples include:

   > To empower people to have meaningful conversations so that, together, we can transform our relationships.
   > To illuminate the path so that we can create possibilities that we never knew existed.
   > To transform purpose into direction, so that we live our lives to the fullest.

   There is a very specific methodology for developing these phrases that requires another party's help, so without going into enormous detail, I'll just note that it's necessary to follow Sinek's instructions. You can read more about the process for developing a WHY statement in his co-authored book *Find Your Why: A Practical Guide for Discovering Purpose for You and Your Team,* or via www.SimonSinek.com.[35]

*   *   *

However you word your life purpose in this initial draft is fine, as long as you feel that it identifies a clearer sense of direction for you. If you've already drafted one in the past, take a few moments to refine what you have so that your draft is current and specific. Above all, remember that we just want to get some words down for now, not necessarily the final version. While you can and should take time to reflect, clarify, and refine your draft, for our purposes, it's important not to stall here indefinitely until you get it just right. (In my case, the iteration process took about six months!) If you find yourself losing momentum at this step, give yourself permission to keep going for now, and revisit your life purpose draft after you've let it sit for a while or you've talked to your supporters about it.

The second half: the more practical way in which you go about accomplishing your life purpose

Next, because this is a *career* purpose, it's important to give some clarification on the ways in which you could accomplish this mission through the work that you do. Two ideas are key here: You'll want to keep this section high-level in order to leave room for many options of roles to accomplish your career purpose—in other words, this is not the place to list specific job titles. And, because you're looking for meaningful and fulfilling work, stick only to what you *enjoy* doing.

Let's go back for a moment to the strengths that you identified in chapter two to help fuel you for the journey. In this half of your career purpose statement, we're going to use that list as a starting point to look for strengths that are *also* leads as defined in our last chapter. (No need to worry too much about terminology here—we'll go through the process together.)

First, how many strengths have you already identified? For this section, I'd recommend working with at least five to ten strengths to give you some options. Remember, these are activities that make time pass quickly for you and make you feel alive; they are not necessarily activities you are skilled at doing. Feel free to revisit chapter two if you need to generate more ideas.

Then, to figure out which strengths are also leads for you, divide your list of strengths into two parts: the strengths you are less interested in being paid to do, and the strengths you are more excited about the thought of being paid to do (and thus don't mind the work it takes to get there). If income is not a primary motivation for you, you could consider which strengths you're more excited about being *responsible* for doing—where people would count on you to provide the work, service, or product within a certain timeframe—or that you'd be most excited to tell people about. These questions will help you separate working activities, regardless of whether they include payment, from the hobbies you enjoy doing whenever you feel like it or have the free time to do them.

Make sure not to write off any strengths under the assumption that you "can't" get paid to do them—only separate out the ones you don't particularly *care* about being paid to do. We are not focusing on immediate practicality at this stage. You can always revise this later, so again, don't worry about getting it perfect.

For the strengths that you're *less* interested in being paid to do (or being responsible for doing), it means that they're probably not leads for you, and, therefore, probably not part of your career purpose. However, please keep these for your free time! They are, after all, fuel. They can be hobbies, volunteer work, side projects, or just activities that you do for fun to recharge. Whether you are skilled at doing them is irrelevant for two reasons: First, you can always gain new skills. And second, just because you're good at doing something that you also happen to enjoy doesn't automatically make it part of your career purpose.

> Just because you're good at doing something that you also happen to enjoy doesn't automatically make it part of your career purpose.

For example, I enjoy crocheting in my free time and am also fairly skilled at the craft after years of practice. It is a strength for me, meaning that it makes time go by quickly and fuels me. While it is *possible* that I could make a living at this strength (there are influencers who do so as spokespeople for particular yarn brands, and there are designers who write high volumes of patterns that generate passive online income), I don't feel any particular sense of excitement about that path, the work that it would take to make it happen, or being responsible to produce finished items or patterns in a certain timeframe. Put in our earlier terms, that means this strength is not a lead for me, and therefore, it is not connected to my career purpose. It is just a hobby and creative outlet that I can use as fuel for the journey, and maybe a little bit of side cash as a bonus.

Next are the activities that give you a sense of *excitement* at the thought of being paid to do (or being responsible for doing); these are excellent candidates for the ways in which you could accomplish your life purpose within the context of your work. These are the activities that are both leads *and* strengths, as coaching and teaching are for me. I am fueled by the activities themselves and enjoy most of the work to find new clients, design workshops, and handle administrative tasks. I feel excited and blessed every single day that I get paid to do them. I take the responsibility for helping my clients grow, learn, and improve their organizations very seriously, and I feel highly fulfilled as I witness their transformations. Put differently, I enjoy both the outcome *and* most of the process it takes to get there.

In your case, let's say that selling is a strength that you're excited about getting paid to do (meaning that it is also a lead for you). You could use this activity as a means to accomplish your life purpose by selling products, services, or even ideas that help people in relation to your life purpose. If teaching is both a strength and a lead for you, then you can find meaning in teaching others, even in a setting as simple as break room conversations. Notice with these two examples that they are broad enough to be something that you could do within any job. As a mentor of mine put it, "You can find purpose in *what* you do or in *how* you do it."

Which activities are both strengths and leads for you? Stick with two to three options for now, and if they don't seem connected to each other, try zooming out a level and considering what it is in common about all of them that fulfills you. If you're still struggling to generate ideas, you can try pulling ideas directly from your list of leads, or if you did Simon Sinek's WHY discovery process, you can see if any of the HOWs you identified are also leads for you. If you're unsure of which ones to pick, recall that the bottom line when seeking fulfillment is always to go with what gives you the strongest positive feeling.

Putting the two halves together

When you put the two halves together, you'll have a life purpose and a way in which you can accomplish it at a high level. Let's look at a few examples of how you can put the two halves together.

In two of the examples from above—the value of adventure as well as the strength (and lead) of teaching—that person might have a career purpose statement that looks something like this when put together: "Find the adventure in every situation *(life purpose)* by teaching people to enjoy the moment *(the way in which they accomplish this purpose)*." The beauty of a statement like this is that you can carry out this purpose in any industry or role—you can be a literal teacher, or you could find teaching moments in any job. The statement does not limit your options; rather, it helps you to know which options are pointing you in the right direction toward a sense of fulfillment.

> The beauty of a statement like this is that you can carry out this purpose in any industry or role.

Here's another example of putting the halves together, based partly on one of my client's stories. The client had, unfortunately, experienced a stressful event during his teen years, after which a mentor who was there for him in his time of need had deeply impacted his life. This gave him a life purpose of "helping people through emotional stress." One of the strengths (and leads) that he chose for the second half of the statement was problem solving, and thus, his career purpose statement is: "to help people through emotional stress by problem solving with them." Today, he is thriving as an employee at a funeral home, helping families solve logistical challenges that they face with their loved one's arrangements.

Notice how this person could also apply this career purpose statement in other roles or industries. That is the litmus test to ask yourself: Could you accomplish *your* drafted career purpose statement in any industry or role? If you got too specific in the second half (for example, "through teaching first-grade students how to write"), try taking out a few of the qualifiers. There are no right answers here, and remember, for our purposes, this exercise should yield a specific draft that gives you direction, not necessarily the final version of the statement. It's okay if your statement feels too long at this stage; we will condense the information in the next chapter.

A few final thoughts about your career purpose statement

How does it feel to see it written down in front of you for the first time? Motivating? Overwhelming? Confusing? However you feel about it, keep your draft statement handy throughout the process of finding your career purpose so that you can always have a reminder of where you're going and what matters most to you on this journey. Feel free to keep tweaking it throughout the process and in consultation with your supporters (they're also a great resource if you're feeling lost or confused in the process). Above all, celebrate it—post it, frame it, share it! This is *your* career purpose statement!

COMPONENT #2: DIVE DEEPER INTO YOUR "IDEAL DAY" EXERCISE

Refer back to the exercise that you did in chapter one in which you visualized in detail what the ideal day of living your career purpose looks like. Here are a few questions to consider that will help you distill important insights out of this exercise:

1. *What aspects do you notice about your routine?*

   How do you start and end your day—journaling, reading, studying, praying or meditating, showering, getting the kids to school, talking to customers or loved ones, exercising ... ? One of the military veterans I shared this exercise with chose to plot his ideal day hour-by-hour as he had done on deployments. A similar systematic approach may help you think of ideas that you might not have considered otherwise about your routine; or, if that idea sounds awful to you, it may be a clue that you thrive with a flexible, unstructured day.

2. *How is your ideal environment different than the one that you have now?*

   Where are you working during your ideal day? Are you traveling more? Spending more time outside? Does your vision include a particular space, such as a desk with lots of light? Open offices where you can interact easily with collaborators? A high rise in an urban setting? Coworking space? Coffee shop? Home office? Are you working solo and thrilled to be able to think in silence, or are you enjoying some lively music while you work in the office with your colleagues?

3. *What other details do you notice about what* **you** *need to feel the most fulfilled?*

   What details stand out that you might not have consciously been thinking about previously? For instance, mine revealed that I am not made for a traditional job sitting at a desk in an office, because I pictured working from a home office while managing my clients and developing my business. I also pictured doing this largely alone, which is not surprising given that I am an only child and an introvert—I am quite comfortable setting my own agenda! These were invaluable clues about what my dream job would entail. Maybe in your case, your pets made an appearance in this exercise, so you know that you want to bring them with you while you work at an outdoor spot on a nice weather day. Or perhaps you pictured skateboarding into the office, which tells you that you are in *no* way meant for a traditional or formal environment (yes, this example is based on a true story!).

What does your description of an ideal day reveal to you? Is there anything missing that you could add—people, environment, structure, schedule, or otherwise? Remember that we'll synthesize this information in the next chapter, so for now, just focus on what insights come to mind without too much judgment of the ideas or pressure to get to a certain volume of them.

If you could use some inspiration on how others just like you have benefitted from this exercise in their career purpose journeys, here are some thoughts that two people I've coached shared with me:

"Most fundamentally, this exercise made the work and life I wanted to create feel 'real' in a way that I had never dared (or felt that I had permission) to fully imagine before. It helped me move from 'I wish I could . . .' to visualizing concretely what I actually wanted to do and how it would feel, which was further underscored in discovering my strengths. The ideal day became easier to call upon as a tangible point of comparison, especially during a day where my activities or priorities were misaligned with my career purpose. Finally, it helped (forced!) me to break out of the mindset that 'work is work,' which opened up a world of possibilities where my 'work' could be a vocation: fun, fulfilling, and energizing."

"The exercise allowed me to focus on questions such as: 'Who do I want to spend my time with?'; 'What do I want my family and friends to say about me when I am gone?'; and 'Where do I want to spend my time?' Once these questions were answered, I moved on to how to make it happen. These iterations have shown me that I have more time than I thought I did to do things other than just work. They have challenged me to identify what is really important to me and not just how I plow through my day and get fifty things knocked off a checklist."

Which parts of these comments resonate most with you? Consider how to put your own spin on this exercise to make it unique to your journey.

Finally, ask yourself which parts of this ideal day you can begin setting up now. Why wait until you're living your career purpose to experience the joy? Many of these aspects may be within your immediate control. If you wrote about more light, go get a lamp from the next room. Now. Worry about what it looks like later. Or, if you wrote about exercising in the mornings, don't wait to start doing so; set an alarm right now to start tomorrow morning—and so on. How many parts of your ideal day can you implement today? Doing so will give you momentum on your path and help you see that there is less distance between where you are now and where you want to be than it may initially seem.

COMPONENT #3: GENERATE KEYWORDS TO USE AS SEARCH TERMS

You can gather keywords from any information about what a job is like— whether you're reading a job description, chatting with someone about what they do, or browsing websites of various for-profit or non-profit organizations. The end goal for having these keywords is twofold: to gather clues about what your dream job is that we'll synthesize in the next chapter; and, if applicable in your situation, to start generating terms you can use to search for jobs.

What keywords have you already identified in the direction of your career purpose? Whether you've actively thought about this or not, you likely have several keywords already. Take a look back through your notes from the exercises in this chapter, or reflect on conversations that you've had about this journey. What terms have emerged? It doesn't really matter how close or far away you are to an exact job title or industry—any words that come to mind will do as a start, and you can refine your searches as you go.

One of my coaching clients identified *organizational development* as an initial term. Through progressively targeted conversations, reviewing job descriptions, taking an executive education course, and even reading a book on the subject called *The Culture Code: The Secrets of Highly Successful Groups* by Daniel Coyle, he was able to identify more keywords: *change management*, *data visualization*, *business model design*, and *transformational design*, to name a few. Because he had narrowed the search before our chat, I was able to connect him with a couple of very targeted colleagues among the hundreds I know in the field, so that he could continue following his leads. He will also use these keywords as search terms when he's ready to apply for positions, whereas if he had stayed with the original *organizational development* as his primary search term, his results wouldn't be nearly as pertinent.[36]

Try it out yourself: Read through job descriptions, peruse organization's websites, or even look in "out-of-the-box" places like photos of people doing the type of work you want to do, and notice what you *feel* as you explore them. You may want to print them out and write in the margins, or assign one color of underlining or font to positive feelings and another color to negative feelings that you get as you see them. What sounds intriguing? What sounds dull? What makes you want to rip it up and never search for that term again? Make sure to focus on things that *excite* or *repel* you. Then, compile the positive and negative items into lists and look for patterns or themes; ask one of your supporters for help if needed. The themes that you notice on your positive list are what go into your list of keywords, and the negative ones serve as a guide or filter for what to avoid as you continue along this process. As with the other components, there is no correct volume or type of keywords here—we are simply collecting information.

COMPONENT #4: GATHER IDEAS FROM INFORMATIONAL INTERVIEWS

I first learned about informational interviews as part of the traditional job search strategy. They are incredibly helpful for building your network, and they can really come in handy when an interesting job opens if these individuals are willing to put in a good word for you or make an introduction to the hiring manager. While this strategy can enhance your chances of garnering an interview, it's not the reason that we're exploring it relative to your career purpose. In terms of the latter, informational interviews give you just that—information—to react to as a component of your career purpose.

This information can come in a few forms:

1. The person you're interviewing may share industries, job titles, or keywords that you can then use for component #3. They often know of terms that you didn't realize existed, which can unlock new information and searches for you to consider.

2. They may relay their own experiences, likes, and dislikes about the field or organization that you can react to and use as leads.

3. They may become a mentor or advocate to help you along your path once they hear what you're interested in and passionate about doing, which can provide access to new and more targeted insights and opportunities.

4. They may tell you about other people you should speak with who can provide additional information about more targeted roles, organizations, or industries for you to consider—and they're usually also willing to connect you to them.

I love this strategy because there's really nothing to lose—the worst that can happen is they turn you down for the conversation, which rarely happens. You'll also be surprised how many of these conversations, which might not seem to be as pertinent at the time, turn into highly valuable relationships years down the road. This has happened to me so many times that I couldn't even count how many. You just never know—which is why I never turned down a single connection during all the years that I was going after my career purpose, and I still strive to meet as many people as I possibly can.

How can you identify people to interview?

Ideas for whom to contact for these informational interviews can come from any of the work that you've done so far to identify your career purpose. Here are examples of how you could go about this: If one of your leads was the culture at a particular organization, reach out to your network to find someone who works at that organization. If you identified a keyword in component #3, search your network or ask your supporters if they know anyone who has that keyword in their job title or responsibilities. If one of the strengths that you identified is writing, think about who you know who's written blogs, books, or news articles. Perhaps your ideal day included data analysis, and your brother works at an IT firm—you could ask him for recommendations for someone to chat with.

For now, keep it simple and identify about three or so initial contacts and send a quick request for a few minutes of their time to learn more about what they do. As long as you continue to pay attention to how you feel about the content of those initial conversations, using the lead-following process we discussed, you'll have clarity about who the next round of more targeted people to contact is.

An example from my own journey

The most solid leads that I had at this point in my journey were: teaching leadership skills, mentoring, and coaching. I wanted to go into a field that focused on these areas, but I didn't know what it was called or how I could search for related careers. Through the process of conducting around twenty to twenty-five informational interviews with people in similar fields, I was able to identify four options to explore: human capital consulting, a position within the talent development team in human resources at a larger company (such as corporate trainer), a human resources rotational program, or starting my own business.

A few keys to success

Informational interviews yield the most helpful information when you get more and more refined as you go. Use your initial few interviews strategically to find more relevant and targeted contacts and to ensure that you reach enough people beyond those in your immediate network; aim for a total of around twenty to thirty interviews overall. One nonprofit organization for which I serve as a volunteer, The Honor Foundation, helps members of the U.S. Special Operations Forces transition to civilian careers. For this career transition process, they suggest the participants complete what they call "fifty cups of coffee." You read that right: fifty! That many meetings will all but guarantee that you will reach people you never would otherwise, and that they will connect you to the best, most targeted people you should be talking to.

If you're not sure how to get started, what questions to ask, or general dos and don'ts of networking, there are tons of books, coaches, classes, and online resources that can teach you about the basic strategies of networking. Just keep in mind that, although the strategies are similar, our goals related to finding your career purpose listed above are slightly different than the usual goals for networking and informational interviews. Lastly, don't forget to lean on your supporters—they could help you think through the best people to speak with or make initial connections for you.

A note to those who are introverted, shy, or both

We all have our struggles in life, and being introverted, shy, or both (yes, they are different!) can make this process difficult for some. Take heart: the more you do it, the more you will get used to it, and it will come more naturally to you. Because we all have challenges on the path to finding our career purpose, I would call this an "excuse" as defined in the last chapter—and I say that from experience, because I happen to be both introverted and shy. Don't allow a situation in which people drain you or cause you anxiety to block you or stall you from finding your career purpose. Do it anyway—you're worth it.

A few final thoughts from a coaching client

In case you're feeling any remaining hesitancy about informational interviews, here are a few thoughts and tips one of my coaching clients kindly shared with me about her experience that may help:

> "I was skeptical at first because I was afraid that by reaching out to people I hadn't spoken to recently, or those who I'd never met, I risked coming across like I was just trying to get a 'foot in the door.' I was also worried that I needed to make sure that I reached out to the 'right' people—those who had roles that I was interested in. Once I started, it was truly a great way to learn about people, their work, and what motivates them. Even roles outside of what I initially thought I'd like were useful to learn from. I found it incredibly helpful to have the structure of three specific questions that I asked across all interviews to hear the ways in which their answers differed. People were also willing to connect me with colleagues, suggest alternate roles, and share feedback based on what I shared with them. Their answers helped me identify clues about what I need in the work and environment of my next role to feel fulfilled."

Which parts of this quote resonate most with you?

You may notice that the quote contains elements of keywords, informational interviews, and the ideal day exercise. These components can sometimes overlap; there's no need to keep it all perfectly boxed into exact categories. Simply focus on gathering information that we can synthesize in the next chapter.

COMPONENT #5: EXPLORE YOUR PERSONALITY TRAITS

One of my favorite ways to help clients generate information about their career purpose is to explore what types of careers other people of their same personality type find fulfilling. We don't all fit into stereotypes about our personalities; thus, this strategy is not intended to limit our options, but rather to give us a "menu" of options from which to choose. Many of the personality tests out there include a career suggestion component to them or have an additional career report that you can purchase. It's so much more helpful to have a list to start from than to generate options from scratch, particularly when you "don't know what you don't know." You can ask a certified practitioner for the personality assessment of your choice whether it includes these career suggestions, or work with a career coach for advice on other career-related assessments that you could take.

Even without a career report in-hand, any personality test (or any personality traits you have that you're already aware of) can shed light onto what you do and don't like, which you can use as data in this component of your career purpose. Here are some examples: If you have a curious and intellectual personality type, you could consider careers in research. If you have an outgoing and bubbly personality type, you may thrive in customer service. Or, if you have a nurturing and gentle personality type, perhaps you would find fulfillment in nursing, counseling, or teaching. What clues does your personality type give toward your career purpose?

* * *

My husband and I used to frequent a particular pharmacy in our community, and I still remember a cashier who worked at the checkout counter there. Every time we came in the door, his face would light up and greet us pleasantly. It wasn't the kind of forced greeting that one typically gets in a retail setting—not that people are trying to be rude, but hopefully you know what I mean when I say that it just sometimes doesn't feel as genuine. This employee's greeting always felt genuine. When we got to the register, there would be that big grin waiting for us. "Mr. President!" he would sometimes call my husband, making us both chuckle. "Find everything you need today?"

How can you *not* smile at that kind of treatment? Even for two introverts, he made us want to come back and talk to him. Occasionally, when I went to the pharmacy during a different shift, I would find a different cashier—a woman with a sullen face. She oozed an "I don't want to be here" vibe. Again, not that she was rude; it was just obviously not someone living her career purpose on the other end of that counter. These two employees could not have a more different demeanor, but they had the same job at the same store. How do we explain this?

While I realize there are many factors at play on a given day as to our demeanor and enjoyment of our jobs, my suspicion is that if we could tap into their thoughts about the work, the first employee might think something like: "I love my job! Every day, I get to meet new people and make them smile." Hearing the same question, the other employee might think something more along these lines: "Every day, I have to go into work and talk to people all day. It feels so exhausting just thinking about it. I wish I could work with spreadsheets—I always loved analyzing data." What if the first was extraverted and the second introverted, and therefore thrived in different kinds of environments? What if one of these employees was living his career purpose every day—a purpose that he could carry out at any number of jobs—and the other was in an environment that was not the right fit for her? Same job, two different personalities, and two different career purposes. Why not go after the job that energizes you?

* * *

What are some of *your* personality traits? Make a note of a few to include in this component of your career purpose. This isn't an exact science, so you can't really get it wrong. You may choose ones from your personality test of choice that seem most pronounced, unique, or that have played a key role in your enjoyment of previous jobs (as the introversion and extraversion in the story above did). Likewise, if you've reviewed careers that people of your same personality type enjoy, include a few that stand out to you here too. Again, we are just collecting information for now.

COMPONENT #6: ADD ANY REMAINING LEADS

Last, but not least—it's time to include the rest of those leads that you identified in chapter three. You may have already included them if they overlapped with other components, so this is just a final catch-all to make sure that we haven't left any pieces out of our inventory. For now, simply put any leads that you haven't already captured together with the other components, and in the next chapter, we'll narrow them down.

WHAT ELSE?

Is there any other information that you feel is important to include in relation to your career purpose? Before you continue, do a quick "gut check" to consider whether anything is missing when you review the components that we've compiled in this chapter: What else could give you a sense of fulfillment in your work? Another option is to show the information that you've collected to a supporter who knows you well, and ask if there's anything else that they feel you should add about who you are at your core or what they've noticed that you enjoy doing.

* * *

It's time to gather all the papers, stickies, notes, and other "puzzle pieces" that you've collected throughout this chapter.

As a quick recap, these may include:

- A draft career purpose statement.
- Insights from your ideal day exercise.
- Keywords to use as search terms.
- Ideas from informational interviews (or at least a request to a couple of people for time on their calendar).
- Personality traits that you've identified about yourself and/or lines of work that people who share your personality type tend to enjoy.
- Any remaining leads from chapter three.
- Anything else that you feel you need to include to feel fulfilled in your work.

If you don't have all of these components, or are experiencing "information overload" at this point, let me be clear that you do *not* have to have 100 percent of the information above to move to the next chapter or to find your career purpose. Some of these components may not resonate with you, and others may take time to gather. I certainly encourage you to go all-out with each exercise, but the most important thing is that you have some ideas that you can build upon, react to, and tweak as you go. Stalling here to gather perfect information is not a license to put off going after your career purpose!

Stalling here to gather perfect information is not a license to put off going after your career purpose!

Next, we'll talk about how to synthesize and refine these components to determine which pieces belong in the "puzzle." That's right: it's time to reveal your dream job(s)!

CHAPTER 5
SYNTHESIZE YOUR COMPONENTS INTO A DREAM JOB

"Far and away the best prize that life offers is the chance to work hard at work worth doing."
— *Theodore Roosevelt*

"Y ou've given us many stellar answers today," the interviewer said near the end of our time together. "You're clearly very bright, came super-prepared, and are capable of doing the job. The only thing I am not hearing from you is excitement specifically for *our* firm."

I paused and hoped she didn't notice my eyes open a little wider as I took in her words.

She was right. I was interested in the idea of human capital consulting as a job in which I could accomplish my career purpose, but I didn't care which firm I worked for.

In that split second, as she looked at me across the table waiting for a response, I had a decision to make. I knew what she wanted to hear, and I could give her that excitement she was looking for. But was that the right thing to do?

I looked back at her. My thoughts flashed forward to working in the job, having to manufacture the same insincere excitement with clients and my colleagues every day that I was about to give her in this interview.

I couldn't do it.

I was here to find my dream job, and I knew in that moment that this opportunity was not it. I realized as the answer was coming out of me (and I have no memory of what I said) that I would be miserable working in a setting in which someone else decided *for* me who the client was, what their problem was, and how I should solve it for them. I realized that I did not want to go to the same client, exclusively, week after week, for the entirety of the engagement with them. I wanted to choose my clients, help them determine what was holding them back, and discover insights together with them for a solution. And I could not do that working for this firm.

I was neither surprised nor disappointed (for long!) when the result came back a day or so later—I had not been selected for the position. This was not my dream job, and I had narrowly escaped work that would drain me.

The next day, I stayed in my office a little while longer after finishing my work for the day. With a fresh cup of decaf in hand, I looked at some job descriptions that I had printed for review. On the surface, they looked perfect. They were in the field that I wanted to go into, had the right salary range, and were much closer to what I wanted to do than where I was. But something just didn't add up. I took a sip of my coffee and leaned in closer. What was giving me a sense of repulsion away from these jobs?

"Director of culture," one of them said. I looked out the window and reflected on the job description for a moment. What would it be like?

"Wait a minute," I thought. The reason this company is hiring for this position is that they are experiencing challenges with respect to their culture. I now realized what I had been missing. I had studied leadership for a few years at this point, and I knew that hiring one person like this would not "fix" an entire organization's culture. Would they bring me into this role expecting as much, be disappointed when I didn't complete an impossible task, and look poorly on my performance?

I looked through the other job descriptions and felt similar feelings. Many of them focused heavily on ROI (return on investment) or metrics. I'm a big believer in setting goals and measuring success, but this felt different. Reading them, I felt like there was such a hyper-focus on the metrics that I would be under a bright light of scrutiny all the time. I pictured reporting to my manager the day after delivering a leadership training and being expected to give a debrief on behavior changes as a result. (Perhaps not literally, but you get the idea.)

With a sigh, I straightened the stack of about twenty-five job descriptions and laid them back down on my desk. Whether I was right about how any particular one of them would turn out, the feelings (leads) that I was getting as I read them served as important clues that indicated they were not the direction that I personally needed to go if I wanted to find work that would be fulfilling to me.

I picked up my belongings and walked out the door to go home. My path was clear to me now. I wanted to teach and coach others, but in my own way—with a lot of flexibility in how I did it, what hours I worked, where I worked, and with whom I worked. I could not personally thrive doing what I wanted to do as an employee within an organization. I needed to start my own business.

*   *   *

As I mentioned in chapter one, I define a "dream job" as one of the points along your career purpose path. As you grow and change along your journey, so will your idea of a dream job. You could have just one idea, or you could have several ideas for jobs that would be dream jobs for you (all the better to have options!). So, how can you identify your dream job(s)?

Going back to our puzzle analogy, this chapter will help you take all the "puzzle pieces" that you gathered from chapter four and synthesize them into one or more dream jobs on a single sheet. This is where you figure out which pieces belong in your puzzle, put them together, and find out what the image is. The best part is that the process doesn't have to end here—you can repeat it each time that you are seeking a new role along your career purpose journey in order to gain clarity along your path!

Compared to the general population, I do not need much structure in my processes. The gift of knowing this about myself is that it means most of you reading this need more structure than I did, and that's the reason for including this chapter. If you're more like me, you may not need to go into this level of detail; like the story above, you might just start exploring some leads.

To help you in this process, we have a free, downloadable worksheet that you're welcome to use at www.CareerPurposeBook.com. Alternatively, you could draw something like Figure 1 in your notes and fill it in on your own:

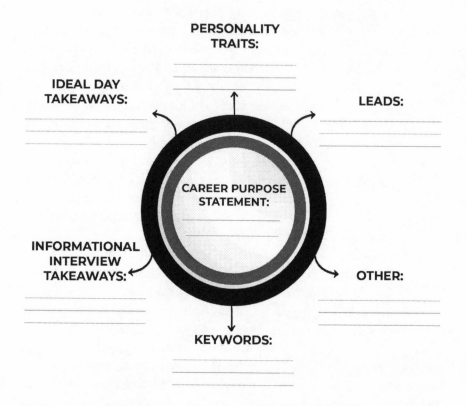

Figure 1. A framework for synthesizing the components of your career purpose into a dream job

WHAT GOES IN EACH SECTION?

To fill in this framework, you'll need to whittle down the components from chapter four into a series of key findings. *This is not the place to list everything—only the few most important details.* Narrowing down these details is the part of our puzzle analogy in which you determine which of the many pieces that you've inventoried actually *do* belong in your puzzle, and, once you have them narrowed down to the right pieces, you will then put them together to determine what the picture on them is—your dream job(s).

Strategies for narrowing down the information

Can you guess by now one of the ways that I would recommend you narrow down the information in your components from chapter four into the key, few words that belong in this framework? That's right—whatever gives you stronger feelings! You can use the same "feelings compass" here to narrow the options that we did from the lead-following process. Whether your career purpose statement needs to be a little more concise, or you have dozens of key-words, or you took pages of notes from the informational interviews, the point at this stage is to clarify which parts give you stronger positive emotional reaction when you see them and put those into the framework (and leave out any that give you negative reactions).

This is not the place to list everything—only the few most important details.

If you're a visual person, try using one color of highlighter or font in your notes for the words that give you the strongest positive emotion when you see them, and another color for anything still remaining that gives you a negative emotion; an example of the latter might be if one of your informational interviewees suggested an idea that you initially wrote down, but now realize that, as you review it and feel a sense of repulsion, it's not right for you.

Another strategy that you could use to narrow down your components from chapter four is to work with your supporters to help you, but make sure you ask the right questions: ask which parts of the components you've gathered that they have seen you *happiest* doing or talking about versus which ones they think you *should* do or that you would be *good at* doing. You could also ask the people from your informational interviews to help you narrow some options based on the specific ideas you're *most* passionate about from your conversations.

Finally, you could "live" the process through trial and error. Let's say you identified that you want to be in a fast-paced environment from your ideal day exercise, but upon experiencing that kind of environment at a friend's company over a lunch meeting, you realize it's too hard to think in that setting for you. Voilà—you have just narrowed your list by living it.

Your turn!

Go ahead and put some initial thoughts into each section of the framework before we continue. Remember, the point is not about whether you have the "right" pieces yet, or which category that you decide to put them in—only that you have a few targeted words and phrases on your page to work with. You can always repeat or refine the process, just as if you accidentally included a puzzle piece that didn't actually belong, you could always take it out later once you realized it doesn't fit. In other words, it's better to just get something down that you can later modify than it is to get stuck in analysis paralysis trying to figure out what to write. A few words or phrases in each section is all you need.

Here's an example of how I could fill in the sections based on my career purpose:

Figure 2. A filled-in example

If you find yourself with important words or phrases to include in your framework, but have questions about which ones belong in which section, just write them down anywhere. The idea is to get the few words and phrases that matter *most* to you out onto one page together, not for them to fit perfectly into this framework.

Here's another real-life example for you based on one of my coaching clients:

Figure 3. Another filled-in example

I FILLED IN EACH OF THE SECTIONS— NOW WHAT?

Once you've narrowed down the words or phrases to a key few, you'll have a much clearer and more targeted view of what your "puzzle image" is. Now, it's time to reveal what that image is for you—let's translate what you've identified into a dream job! Here are a few suggestions for how to do this:

Identify common themes and patterns

Now that you've narrowed down the information, it's time to look at it all together on one, single sheet. Often, if you're trying to process large amounts of information like we had in chapter four, this step can become daunting and it can be really hard to see the patterns. (Just as it would be harder to figure out what puzzle you're putting together if you have many pieces from other puzzles that don't belong.) But now, you have a more targeted list of items in your framework and are more likely to be able to see those patterns. Are there themes among your different pieces? What picture is emerging? There is a place to note these on our downloadable worksheet, or you can simply make a list of themes and patterns in your notes.

> The only "right" answers are whatever prospects feel the most exciting to you.

As an example, let's look back at Figure 3. While there are numerous ways (by design) to distill a dream job out of this information, the only "right" answers are whatever prospects feel the most exciting to you. Some terms that stand out to me are: *stories, legal research, serving people, problem solving,* and *mental and physical health.* So, dream jobs could include anything from a copywriter for a law firm whose blog helps clients solve problems that they may be facing to an advisor who helps kids gain access to mental health resources they need as part of their school counseling programs. There are so many possible answers since we can accomplish our career purpose in any role or industry; if you can just generate one or more ideas for now, you can start exploring them, modify the list as you learn more about each potential path, and follow leads accordingly.

Need another example? Let's say your framework has the following words and phrases on it: *curious about how things work; like to fix things; ideal day is on my feet, not at a desk all the time; love helping people; value health and well-being.* A possible dream job could be managing a team of employees in a factory or warehouse for a nutrition or fitness company, where, every day, you get to help your employees troubleshoot issues with the machines, knowing that your work ultimately leads to the customers becoming healthier as a result of the products they buy from your team. (This would be a great description to take back to your informational interviewees for help identifying a target company or role to explore further.)

Get input

Grab some names off your list of supporters—or a mentor, loved one, friend, coach, or any of the people who stood out to you from your informational interviews—and show them your framework. Of note, this is a different process than asking them for help narrowing your options for what to put in the framework. To use our puzzle analogy, the narrowing part helps you figure out which pieces do and do not belong in your puzzle, whereas *this* input is to help you figure out what the image on your puzzle is. What patterns or themes do the people you show your framework to notice?

If you've ever experienced that feeling of looking at a document for so long, or reading it repeatedly, that you can no longer see information staring you in the face, you'll know what I mean when I say that the value of a fresh perspective to help you connect the pieces cannot be understated here. Outside input is also critical if you have a general idea of what you want to do, but you need help identifying a more specific job title or industry, as we saw in the previous example about the idea of a potential role within a nutrition or fitness company.

Ask yourself, "Who has a job like this, or where have I seen something like this before?"

Chances are, you've come across *something* similar to the image emerging from your puzzle pieces. Think back over your lifetime—who have you known in a similar role, industry, environment, company, team, or culture? Whom do you know from your family, colleagues, classmates, mentors, direct reports, neighborhood, religious or spiritual community, social media, historical figures, or even fictional characters that the parts of your framework remind you of? One way to answer this is to look through your framework systematically and ask yourself these questions with each word or phrase. Ask yourself: "Whom do I know who's studied engineering or been an engineer?"; "Whom do I know who's worked in a quick-service restaurant?"; "Whom do I know who's really good at public relations?"; "Where have I seen a job that combines finance and creativity before?"; and so on. You can then use this information as clues that you can explore further.

State the obvious

Occasionally, I have clients who do this exercise and find all indications leading to one answer that they struggle to acknowledge. Have you ever heard of the "duck test?" Namely: If it looks like a duck, swims like a duck, and quacks like a duck, then it probably is a duck. So, why do we sometimes struggle to call it a "duck?"

You may recall that what holds us back from doing the work that we truly love is our limiting beliefs and fears. It would be understandable, then, for you to experience a subconscious resistance to acknowledging the truth that is emerging from your framework—you might feel more comfortable, competent, stable, or safe by not acknowledging it. For example, if you have a fear of the unknown, then a resistance to acknowledging your dream job (whether intentional or not) allows you to stay "safe" in the comfort of what you know.

I have a colleague who told me about his dream job a few years ago, and every time we've spoken since then, he speaks about his career path as if he's still trying to figure out what his dream job is. It feels to me like there's always a reason why he can't go after it, so he keeps searching and searching for the next best step instead. What would you say to him if you were me? (I ask because the answer might help you if you're experiencing something similar.) We love to see people happy and thriving, but of course nobody can *make* anyone go after their dream job. So, a great starting point is simply bringing any resistance to your awareness if this is something you are experiencing.

If all indications are pointing to one industry or role and you find a sense of resistance in your mind, could you, too, be steering away from your dream job—consciously or not? If so, why? Is there an aspect of it—risk, change, the unknown—that scares you? Is it possible that you could be trying to explain away your fear with logical reasons not to go after that kind of role? We will address these fears and limiting beliefs in chapter seven; for now, the idea is simply to acknowledge if they might be at play. This could be your dream job staring you in the face. It's okay if you're not ready to stare back yet (or immediately go after it), but acknowledging what it is serves as a critical first step.

IDENTIFY YOUR NON-NEGOTIABLES

One of my favorite workshop topics to teach is negotiations. In negotiations strategy, there is a concept called "reservation price" or "reservation point." Simply put, this term represents the maximum or minimum you're willing to accept—whether monetary or any other factors—in a negotiation before you walk away without reaching a deal. So, what does this have to do with your dream job? For our purposes, I'll call these factors your "non-negotiables."

As you synthesize the components from chapter four, notice which words or phrases give you the *strongest* overall reaction or feeling. These strongest factors will be your non-negotiables: the factors that, if you have too much of them or not enough of them (or if they are present or absent, as the case may be), it will mean that a job you are considering is not a dream job for you. These non-negotiables will serve as a critical filter to give you clarity as you consider various roles.

I'll give you an example from my journey: Flexibility is one of my non-negotiables. I absolutely could not *stand* going to the same desk, in the same office, for the same hours, day after day after day when I worked in traditional jobs. I needed a minimum change of scenery and activity every now and then as well as the freedom to do non-work-related activities in the middle of the day (such as exercising at the warmest part of the day in the winter months). For me, flexibility is a non-negotiable for a dream job, because if I have all the other components that I love, but am stuck at a desk all day, day after day, it will ruin the feeling of fulfillment for me.

For you, it may be the culture or environment in which you work, or the type of colleagues, customers, or manager you work with, or aligning your values with your work, or a certain way you must structure your day in order to thrive—only you know what these factors are for you. Just like the reservation point in negotiations, if taking the job means not meeting these requirements that are critical to your sense of fulfillment, then it is a "no deal" on the path to your career purpose.

One note of clarification here: Your non-negotiables should be based on what will get in the way of your *feeling of fulfillment*, not based on logistical or other factors. For instance, if you need to work certain hours so that you can pick up the kids, that's very important, but it's a separate conversation (and probably something you could work out with the hiring manager). It would be unlikely to ruin your *feeling of fulfillment* not to work those hours. Your non-negotiables are factors that would ruin that feeling for you if the requirements weren't met.

Knowing what these non-negotiables are will help you filter out jobs that won't be dream jobs as you consider the options available to you. If you come

across an exciting prospect, but it doesn't meet your non-negotiable requirements, then having clarity on what your non-negotiables are makes it easier
to know when a job is not the right fit for you.

Make a note for now of any ideas that you have for what your non-negotiables are in your notes or on our worksheet. Lastly, if you can't think of any
right now, that's okay too—just notice as you go through the process if you
have especially strong feelings about an aspect of a job as you're reading
descriptions, interviewing, talking to people who work at the organization,
and so on.

CLAIM IT!

Woohoo! Once you have all the pieces together and have thought about
what your dream job(s) could be, write it down. (Yes, there is a place on our
worksheet for that too.) Whatever you do, don't let them stay in your head.
Tell your supporters. Own it. Get excited about doing these jobs! I'm not
just trying to encourage you by say-
ing that; research on the psychological principle of consistency suggests
that you'll be significantly more likely
to take bigger actions later—in our
case, going after your dream job—if
you make these smaller types of com-
mitments now (particularly if you do so "publicly" to your supporters).[37]

Keep in mind that, the stronger the positive emotions you feel when you
think about transitioning to a job in the area you've identified, the more likely it is that you have found exactly what you're meant to do. If you could still
use some help, go back to your supporters or people from the informational
interview process to find out what "the" job is that your framework reveals.

> Tell your supporters.
> Own it. Get excited about
> doing these jobs!

WHAT IF YOUR DREAM JOB DOESN'T FIT NEATLY INTO AN EXISTING ROLE?

What if your dream job doesn't currently exist?

If you feel like your dream job doesn't exist, my first question is almost always
"Are you sure?" (to confirm that this is not an excuse not to go after it in
disguise). If the answer is yes, you've done your due diligence and you're sure

that it doesn't currently exist, I know how you feel! That was what I found to be the case, too . . . but that is still not an excuse not to go after it. *Make the job you want.* Easier said than done, I know, but it can be done. I'm living proof—I started my own business, and with time, found clients and grew the business to a point where my everyday work both pays the bills *and* is immensely fulfilling to me.

If you have done all the work to narrow your options, conducted informational interviews, reviewed current job descriptions, and still cannot find a way to get into your dream job, then one option that you could explore is self-employment. How to go about doing so (and how and when to make the leap) is another book entirely; fortunately, there are tons of resources out there to help you. You can read books; take classes; download templates online for business plans, financial forecasting, marketing plans, etc.; watch videos; or conduct informational interviews with freelancers, contractors, and entrepreneurs. If you're in the United States, one place that you can start with is the many free or low-cost county, state, university, and federal resources for small business owners. In some cases, mentorship programs and funding are available, too. Don't forget to leverage your supporters and your network to help you along the way. With all the help available to you, the most important thing that you ultimately need is the desire and passion to make it happen. If I did it, so can you!

*Note: We'll discuss strategies in the next chapter that you can use if something **close** to your dream job exists, whether it's a similar role that you could make some tweaks to or an ideal organization or team in which you could propose a new role.*

Can you find your dream job on a non-traditional path or post-retirement?

Absolutely! In fact, that's the reason I named my business Flourishing Work instead of Flourishing Work*place*. Your dream job does *not* have to be in a traditional workplace setting. It is whatever work you feel that you are meant to do, regardless of where it is or how it looks. You can even find and live a "career" purpose *after* retirement, in which case, not only would it not be too late to find it, but it could also very well be the perfect opportunity to have the freedom and space to do so.

Earlier, I stated that a career purpose is the way in which you go about accomplishing your life purpose through work that you typically would do in exchange for income, but if you're blessed with a situation in which income is not a primary driver or need for you, then you can certainly still do meaningful work. This work could be in the form of volunteering; taking care of your home, kids, or grandkids; community involvement; hobbies; and so on.

I've known several stay-at-home parents who thrived in that role full-time and worked out a way to do so, and others who felt a desire to use their other gifts (such as providing clinical care or administrative support) and found great meaning in doing work outside of the home, too. A "career" purpose is all about a life of fulfilling work, and the dream jobs along that journey can take any form as long as you feel that you're doing the work that you're meant to do.

One point of clarification that I'll make is the distinction between work that you love doing and work that enables you to do other things. Network marketing, passive income strategies, and investing are examples of income generators that do not necessarily involve going to a workplace during standard hours. Could they be dream jobs for you? Of course—*if* you love these types of work and thrive in them, then they can give you a sense of meaning and purpose. That is different than doing these types of work only because they allow you to spend time with family through flexible hours or to do other personal activities that you enjoy. It is an understandable strategy; if you don't enjoy the work, why not do fewer hours on a non-traditional path? As we've seen, though, you can make a living at whatever you're passionate about, if you want to; so, unless these types of work fulfill you, they are not part of your career purpose.

HOW DO YOU KNOW WHEN YOU GOT IT "RIGHT?"

It's a bit of a trick question—we're never really done with this process. You could iterate on this framework for the rest of your life and still not get it perfect, so it's more important to go after what you know now rather than to get stuck working on the parts that you're not sure about.

One reason is that, even when you identify your dream job, it can evolve as you pursue it. At this point in my own journey, I had narrowed my options down to one dream job—starting my own business—which, at the time, only consisted of one-on-one coaching services. Once I quit my job to go after that dream, the job immediately evolved from there. When I opened the "doors" of my new business, something unexpected happened. I didn't have many coaching clients; instead, I started getting a lot of requests to give talks. This was perplexing to me because I had neither advertised speaking as a service that I provided nor had the amount of speaking experience that I *thought* I would need to formally offer this service. Without clarity on what my career purpose was, I could have questioned my choice and risked not doing the work that I loved because it didn't perfectly match the coaching dream job that I had gone after.

Because I *was* clear on my career purpose, however, these requests were no-brainers for me, as they still accomplished that purpose, just not in the way that I originally envisioned. That's why it's so critical for your career purpose to be broad and not role-specific. As new clients came my way, all I did was keep following my leads to make sure that each opportunity matched my career purpose before I agreed to them. Over time, patterns emerged for the types of services that my clients were requesting, and I was able to rename my business to encompass my new main service offerings. It turned out that I really enjoyed facilitating, and now it's part of my dream job! Most importantly, I would never have been able to visualize my current dream job from day one as an entrepreneur—and I am sure that by the time you read this, my business and dream job will have evolved even further (and will continue to do so).

The goal at this point is for the job(s) that you have identified in your framework to give you the sense of meaning and purpose that you wanted that drove you to read this book. Ultimately, that's how you know when you've found the first dream job in your career purpose journey, and the next dream jobs along the path will reveal themselves as you continue relentlessly following your leads.

WHAT'S NEXT?

Once you've filled in some targeted words and phrases into this framework, and have identified direction toward one or more possible dream jobs, your next step is to start exploring the types of jobs that have emerged. You may have exact job titles and can start interviewing the way that I did in the opening story of this chapter, or you might need to refine and explore a little further through conducting more informational interviews, continuing to research, or asking for more outside input from a career coach, mentor, or supporter.

The goal is to have at least a few concrete ideas for direction so that you can begin the transition to go after them in the next chapter. It's okay if the ideas are not yet fully formed; as long as you have a direction, you can identify some transition steps. If you do not feel you are at that point, you may need to spend some more time in this chapter and the previous one, or you could continue reading so that you're aware of what the upcoming transition steps will be.

> Your path is unique to you, and what's most important is to keep moving forward on it.

Most importantly, keep going—don't let an absence of complete information serve as a convenient excuse not to continue on the path! If you're feeling stuck, ask yourself: What is one, next step you could take? Any step, no matter how small, will help you gain momentum. As always, don't forget to lean on your supporters if you need to.

Wherever you are on the path is okay; we do not all move at the same speed, nor do we start or end at the same place. Your path is unique to you, and what's most important is to keep moving forward on it.

PART III

LIVING YOUR CAREER PURPOSE

CHAPTER 6
TRANSITION FROM WHERE YOU ARE TO WHERE YOU'RE GOING

"The way to get started is to quit talking and begin doing."
— *Walt Disney*

The fear was crippling me. Everything in me was screaming "Stay with the 'safe' reality that you know! Don't make any changes—the unknown is risky!"

I knew this voice. I had heard it before. And I had conquered it before. So, why, as I was preparing to give my notice a second time in my journey to leave my job for a leap into the unknown, did I still have so much fear? One would think that, having done it once, it would be easier the second time.

While fear can be a biological gift that keeps us safe in many situations, it can also hold us back unnecessarily. Back when the threat was a saber tooth tiger chasing us, fear was quite a helpful response to keep us alive, but when it comes to making a leap of faith in your journey, as long as you're making a responsible decision, fear can keep you from the work that you're meant to do.

This is what I realized in that moment, as the day that I had planned to put in my notice drew nearer and the feeling of fear grew. It became less and less rational as time went on; in fact, my husband and I laid out every possible logical scenario of what could go wrong and what we would do to mitigate the risk. When we finished this exercise, it was clear to me that the only thing holding me back from taking this next important step in my path was fear.

What did I do? In the end, what impacted me the most was asking myself one question: one day, when people tell my story, do I want it to be the version where I took the leap of faith, or the version where I delayed (or worse, where I didn't act at all)? I realized that, because I knew that I would ultimately be okay, my choice was actually one between faith and fear. I decided at that point that I wanted people to tell the version of my story where I chose faith, and that I chose it without hesitation. I could have waited a few months to put in my notice, but I did it that week.

*   *   *

Now, it's your turn to start making the transition (which may or may not include a job change; we'll discuss that shortly). Remember to enjoy the moment—you've found your career purpose, and now all that's left to do is go after your dream job!

Easier said than done, right? Let's explore what the transition to make your dreams a reality looks like. As you read through this chapter, make sure to have your favorite note-capturing tool available to document your thoughts, and focus on identifying a couple of immediate next steps. As you may recall, we will not be covering traditional job-searching strategies such as interview practice, résumé writing, and salary negotiation. Therefore, if you are unfamiliar with these strategies, or need to enhance your skills in these areas, now is a great time to contact a career coach or mentor, investigate career transition programs, or review online resources or books. These resources can also be helpful if you feel stuck, need clarity, or have trouble deciding on next steps during the transition process. Before you continue, is there anything specific you know you need help with that you can make a note of?

STARTING THE TRANSITION

Speak with your supporters

Have you spoken with the people on your list of supporters about your new path? How did they react? Many people experience mixed reactions from others when they start sharing big ideas like going after their career purpose. Some friends and family are excited and happy for you, and others may allow their own insecurities to surface when you speak to them. That's why it's important to focus on your supporters at this stage. They are the group who will cheer you on, be excited for your new journey, and offer to help you through the transition.

Build a "personal brand" around your career purpose

Now that you know what your career purpose is, it's time to be associated more with it in the minds of those around you so that opportunities can come to you organically.

Let's start with what you're *currently* known for. How do people introduce you? What do people ask for your advice about? What meetings, emails, and messages are you included (and not included) on? You can also ask people outright what you're known for. The answers to these questions will help you gauge what your brand currently is, so that you can move more purposefully toward one associated with your newfound career purpose.

Here are a few ways that you can go about modifying your brand to align with your career purpose:

- As you converse with people throughout the day, talk more about what you *love* doing, and people will naturally feel your energy about it.

- Update your professional social media profiles with the words and phrases you selected in chapter five, as well as your profile and cover photos, to align with your career purpose. In our example earlier, where someone's career purpose has to do with adventure, that person could put their favorite travel photo as their cover photo and enter the keywords about languages or destinations they want to be associated with throughout their profile.

- Allocate more of your time and energy to people, teams, or meetings related to your career purpose, when possible.

- Volunteer to help with projects—both inside and outside of your current work environment—that align more with your passions.

- Seek opportunities to move away from tasks or meetings that don't align with your career purpose, when possible.

- Emphasize the words or phrases in your résumé or professional online profiles that align with your career purpose, and downplay or delete those that don't. The idea is to tell a clear and consistent "story" to recruiters, hiring managers, prospective clients, etc.

People can't read your mind, so help them understand what you're passionate about.

People can't read your mind, so help them understand what you're passionate about. I can't tell you the number of opportunities to live my career purpose (read: clients) that I've gotten simply by posting frequently online about what I do and how much I enjoy it!

Apply and interview to help you narrow the list

If your dream job (or jobs) that you identified in chapter five have an application and interview process, it's time to start these (if you haven't already). Neither applying nor interviewing means you *have* to take a job; rather, they will help you continue to narrow your options and leads if you're not yet ready to move. Whether you are exploring a target company, role, environment, culture, boss, team, or something else, the application and interview process is a great way to cross possible dream jobs off your list and get to the one meant for you.

Keep in mind that not every position is open at all times. If the role you desire isn't currently available, you can set up a job search alert so that you're in the loop when such a role opens. More importantly, stay in touch with people in the industry or organization, as they are likely to know about a need or upcoming position well before it is posted.

Note: It may go without saying, but information spreads quickly, so make sure that you're only speaking about this to people whom you trust will keep your search in confidence so as to protect your current role.

Begin any credentialing, certifications, licenses, or other logistical pieces you need

Based on the dream job(s) you've identified, what other next steps do you need to complete to be ready to make the transition? Do you need to build savings, apply for an LLC or contact potential investors for your new business, move to a new location, get certified in anything, or take some night classes? If you're not clear what the first steps are, go back to the people with whom you did informational interviews in your targeted area, and ask what you're missing before you can make the transition. Take a moment to write some thoughts down and make a plan for how you'll start.

One note of caution: be careful not to confuse next steps with an excuse to delay the transition. Before you do anything that will cost significant time or money, ask your network if you *really* need that step. For instance, several of my clients have told me that they thought they needed an MBA to start a business. Heavens, no! Having an MBA myself, I can attest to it being a highly valuable degree for many circumstances, but you do not *need* one to start a business.

> "Wherever you go, go with all your heart." — *Confucius*

Occasionally, we can convince ourselves that we need a certain extra step for plenty of logical reasons, when really, these are just rationalizations for avoiding the real step that we need to take. To test if your idea for a next step might actually be an excuse in disguise, ask yourself: Deep down, what is the reason that you are pursuing this next step? Do you *really* need to do it? Are there any underlying beliefs or fears that could account for the true reason that you're not pursuing the most important next step (for example, feeling unworthy or a fear of risk)? As always, test your assumptions.

ONCE YOU ARE READY (OR ALMOST READY) TO MAKE THE LEAP

Review your finances

Going after your career purpose may involve a potentially scary or risky step like quitting a job or having a few gap months between jobs. Before you dive headfirst, have you set yourself up for success? Conventional wisdom teaches us that we need around six months of salary saved up just in case, and while that is sage advice, I would propose that there is no one-size-fits-all answer. The question, in my opinion, is not what amount of funds that you have saved, but whether you have a solid, responsible plan for this transition. You and your loved ones know your situation best. For some, it may mean taking out a loan, and for others, that would set you up for feeling so much pressure to pay it back that it would distract you from your mission. Some may thrive by cutting all unnecessary expenses, and others may fare best by moving in with a friend or family member temporarily. Evaluate the options that you have, speak with a financial advisor or mentor, and create a reasonable and responsible plan of action.

If you're struggling to act, or you find yourself coming up with all the reasons why you shouldn't or "can't," ask yourself whether you might actually be rationalizing a fear of something such as risk, change, or the unknown. These are very common with my clients who need to make a financial change to go after their dreams. Why? Because income can be intricately woven together with our sense of security (it pays for basic needs like food and housing). Once I ask my clients what the worst-case scenario is and they put words to it, it never sounds as bad out loud as they've been telling themselves it is in their head. Sure, it will involve change or discomfort. However, many meaningful changes in life come with scary decisions, or we would have already done them. The key is to do your diligence to set yourself up for the best chance of success, and at some point, you just have to "jump and grow your wings on the way down."

I am not advocating that you take out a huge loan to buy that food truck that you've always wanted if you're sitting on a mountain of credit card debt. Please consult a professional financial advisor if you need advice in this area or clarification on what a "responsible" plan entails for your unique situation; this book is not intended to be a substitute for professional financial advice.

As one career coach said to me, the sense of security that comes from having a responsible financial plan—even if it will be uncomfortable for a while—may be the key to giving you the ability to jump. In my case, that was completely true. The first (and scariest) time that I made the leap, I spent the weekend prior to giving my notice reviewing all of my monthly income and expenses with my husband. Would our finances be tight for a while when I quit my job? Absolutely. Would we have to make some fairly big and scary changes to our living situation and lifestyle? Yes. Would we survive? Also yes. In fact, once I moved past the fear, I was pleasantly surprised to find that I didn't miss any of the things that I had been afraid to change or lose—it turns out that they all paled in comparison to the joy of fulfilling work. They weren't buying happiness; they were buying an avoidance of my fear.

Speak with the members of your inner circle

This section is intentionally separate from the one suggesting that you speak with your supporters. By "inner circle," I'm referring to those who will be most affected by your transition to fulfilling work. These may be people living in your home with you, immediate family members, or close friends. Remember, they may not be on your list of supporters (which is okay!), and many people are uncomfortable with change no matter how much they care about you. Do not let their reactions automatically deter you if they are unfavorable at first. Give them grace, be patient with them, and help them understand how this move will be a positive one.

Change can be hard for anyone, and they may take some time to process it. Know that those who truly care about you almost always come around in support of positive changes in your life. The main point is to make sure that people who will be affected by this change are not blindsided when you make the leap, and that, to the extent possible, they are on board with it.

Recognize when you need a "stepping-stone"

The path to your career purpose is very unlikely to be linear. Sometimes, you need to step backwards or sideways along the path in order to get where you're going.

Let's say that you discover that your dream job is being a primary care doctor. Obviously, you can't just do that tomorrow—you will have to go to medical school and complete a residency first. Even for jobs that don't require specialized skills or credentials, most people don't go into their dream job right after their education concludes; the path typically includes time for exploration and experience. In my case, I needed time in roles with both good and not-so-good leaders, as well as the experience of managing a team, before I was able to coach individuals and teach workshops on interpersonal and leadership skills. You definitely would not want to see me try to do that right after I graduated from high school (boy, what a funny thought!).

Stepping-stones can provide time for us to build a financial foundation, help us gain more skills or clarity as we live the lead-following process, or serve as a back-up plan if we don't have everything that we need right away. One of my stepping-stones was the part-time job that I mentioned earlier that I had while building my business in the other part of my time. This allowed me to grow my audience, gain confidence, and practice my craft while still maintaining some income and other benefits.

I would encourage you to think creatively about how to fit the pieces together along the path, rather than focusing on a black-and-white or "this-or-nothing" kind of thinking. There may be twists, turns, disappointments, growth spikes, curve balls, and all kinds of other messy pieces on your career purpose journey, as in life. All you need to focus on is momentum: keep your focus on your dream, relentlessly follow the leads that you have, and your path will emerge.

If you aren't sure whether you would need a stepping-stone on your journey, or what that stepping-stone would be (job, degree, credential, skill development, etc.), try asking the people with whom you've conducted informational interviews what else you need to be more marketable for the industry, role, or organization that you're interested in. And—you guessed it—pay attention to how you feel about their advice.

> Stepping-stones don't last forever. They are a means to accomplish the plan.

One disclaimer I would offer is that there is a big difference between taking a less-than-perfect job while you build your plan to go after your dream job, with a clear goal and exit strategy, versus resigning yourself to do work that you don't enjoy because "that's life." Stepping-stones don't last forever, and they are definitely not *the* plan—they are a means to accomplish the plan. Make sure that you are not calling a role a "stepping-stone" while settling for less and using it as an excuse not to go after your career purpose.

Find your dream job where you already are

Is it always necessary to quit your current job to go after your dream job? Of course not! Remember, you can find fulfillment in *what* you do (as I do currently with coaching and facilitation) or in *how* you do it (as I did by coaching the team that I led when I was a manager in a former role). You may have clarified what your career purpose is and feel that you're either in the right organization or in the right role, but just need to make some tweaks for it to be the "dream" job. Great!

Make tweaks to your current role

What if you're fairly happy in your current role, but want to implement some tweaks using your newfound clarity of career purpose? Or, could you use some extra energy for a difficult or draining role while you're working toward another position on your career purpose journey? In their *Harvard Business Review* article, "Managing Yourself: Turn the Job You Have into the Job You Want," Wrzesniewski and co-authors suggest an exercise that they call "job crafting" to bring more of the work that you love doing into your current role. Their framework walks readers through a process to map and re-imagine various aspects of a role, including tasks, relationships, and perceptions.[38]

An abbreviated version of this exercise is to ask yourself: If you could change anything about your job, what would it be? Which colleagues might you want to work with more in order to bring out the best in you? Which team members might you want to delegate a task to so that you can focus more on the items only you can do? What extra projects or initiatives could you take on that you're passionate about?

This strategy helps us test the assumption that "the job is the job" and encourages us that, with a little creative thinking, we can identify tweaks to the scope, nature, or environment of our role in a way that not only fulfills us more on an individual level but also helps improve our performance to benefit the organization.

If you want to make bigger changes that would require approval, or if you'd like to brainstorm ideas with your manager, make sure that you frame that conversation in terms of the value that your suggestions will bring to the team, organization, and the people it serves. That way, it has more potential to be a no-brainer for them to support your ideas. Most managers I've interacted with are willing to at least *hear* your ideas, especially if you approach them with respectful consideration of their priorities and goals.

Two of my recent coaching clients at a global company had great success with this strategy. They both had ideas for initiatives that they could lead in their respective departments. We talked through how their ideas could bring value to the team and the company before they pitched the ideas to their managers. In one case, the manager liked the idea so much that he made the new initiative a *requirement* for other employees to participate in. My client enjoyed leading the process and hearing positive feedback that ensued from the employees who participated. In the other case, my client's manager just so happened to be having conversations with *his* leader about a similar project, so my client was able not only to implement his own idea, but also participate in the additional, similar project. As a result, both clients have incorporated more of the work they love into their current jobs, benefitted the organization, and demonstrated leadership and initiative in the process.

One career coach I spoke with added the following caveats: be intentional about how you prepare for and approach this conversation to be sure your manager is open to the conversation and that you come across the way that you intend. Express gratitude for the opportunities that you've had, and take into consideration the needs of your manager, team, and organization. Do not hesitate to seek advice from a mentor or career coach before having this conversation if you feel you need to run some ideas by them first.

Move to a different—or newly created—role within the same organization

If you love working for the organization that you're currently in, but find through this book that your dream job is a different role, then why leave a good organization? Why not instead sell your value and what you bring to the organization to move internally into a job you love? The easiest path would be if a dream role currently exists and is open for applications, but you can also use the time to build your skills and connections in preparation for when the role does open, or you can work toward building a case for creating a brand-new role.

A colleague and fellow facilitator of mine inspired me to include this idea. She is a corporate trainer within a non-profit organization and loves where she works; however, she saw the opportunity to move into a role that better suited her passions. With help of a mentor, she created a pitch to deliver in the context of her annual performance review conversation, collaborated with her manager and HR to create a new role that aligned the needs of the organization with her passions, and is now happily settled into her new role.

> If you don't have the conversation, then your chances of success are zero percent.

Is it time for you to talk through your ideas with your manager or mentor? If you don't have the conversation, then your chances of success are zero percent. The same career coach advice and caveats from the last section on making tweaks to your role apply here, too. Make sure that you prepare adequately for this conversation and remember to mitigate risk as we discussed.

Test your assumptions before leaving your current job

Have you identified through this process that your current job is not the right place for you to be in order to live your career purpose? If so, great— that level of clarity alone is worth celebrating!

Sometimes, when I speak about my path, people say "You inspire me to want to quit my job!"—but that is *not* what I'm trying to do. Whether or not you have another position lined up, I would never recommend leaving a job (especially not abruptly) without careful consideration. Nor is leaving your current position the only option; as we've seen, other creative options include making tweaks to your current role, pitching a new role within your current organization, taking part-time work while freelancing on the side, and so on.

However, if you've done your due diligence, consulted with loved ones, reviewed your financial situation, have a plan, and are sure that it is the responsible next step on the path to your career purpose, then you should not let fear be the *only* reason that you are held back from taking that next step. And believe me, fear is by far the most common reason that the people I've spoken with over the years have stopped short of going after their dream job at this point in the process.

As we explored in the beginning of this chapter, the fear is there for good reason—to make sure that you are safe or don't make major mistakes—and our task on the career purpose journey is to make sure that it doesn't hold us back unnecessarily. How can you make an informed decision?

You may recall that one of my favorite strategies is to test your assumptions. With that in mind, I compiled a few of the common assumptions I have run across that you can test before making the decision to leave:

Common assumption #1: The grass is always greener on the other side

There are downsides to every job—yes, even your dream job. You could end up trading one pain point for a different one, or finding the new situation is actually worse than the one you had. Don't get me wrong—the new job might very well be better; my only point is to make a more informed decision by testing this assumption. Try interviewing for the new job, talking to people who work for the organization about what it's like, or browsing reviews posted online by current and former employees or customers. If you do get an offer but don't feel like it's the right organization for you, you could always use it to negotiate a raise where you currently are and leverage the job-crafting strategy mentioned previously to find more fulfillment until you identify the right job for you.

A few years ago, a colleague told me a story about how she negotiated a "trial week" as part of a job offer that she received. Everything looked promising about the position, but she hadn't gotten a clear enough picture of what the people were like at this organization. The agreement was that she would begin working in the position and, after one week, would make the final decision about whether she would stay. In the breakroom on her first day, she witnessed two of her new colleagues fighting in a way she described as "childlike immaturity," and she knew instantly this was the wrong fit for her. While you don't have to take this kind of approach and should use discretion in your negotiations, the lesson in this story is that by making sure the "grass" was really "greener" before she formally joined the organization, my colleague saved herself from taking a job that seemed great at first, but in reality, was a poor fit for her. This allowed her to open her options back up to organizations and roles that would be more fulfilling for her.

Common assumption #2: Higher salary means greater fulfillment

Making more money can be an extremely tempting reason to leave your job, but higher salary does not mean more fulfilling work. Of course, if you can be paid more to do what you love, that is wonderful and please go for it! My point is to do a gut check to make sure that you're not considering a move *just* for the money, while potentially entering into a worse situation.

One of my coaching clients told me about a very well-paying job prospect that he had identified. (For context, this particular client was not in a situation at that time in which he needed additional income to make financial ends meet.) As we talked through the possibility, he told me that his wife had cautioned him against taking the role, because she knew that it would be very stressful for him. Yet the temptation of the higher salary—and the added financial stability it would provide for the family—was so strong, it had gotten confused in my client's mind with a sense of fulfillment. When we untangled those pieces together through our session, he realized that the extra income was not worth the effects on his health and the strain that it would put on his family if he were to come home stressed every day. It was then an easy decision.

Common assumption #3: It is always necessary to escape from difficult people or situations

One of my coaching clients was in a low-stakes, temporary position. Her boss was frustrating to work for and constantly failed to provide clarity about the role. It was chaotic, uncomfortable, and full of conflict. Sounds painful and like a great situation to leave, right? However, if we back up a step and look at the bigger picture, a few insights emerge. First, people we find to be "difficult" can be anywhere (sorry!). Would moving to another job *guarantee* all pleasant interactions? Certainly not. Second, given this was a low-stakes, temporary role, what if it were the opportunity of a lifetime to practice working with someone difficult, so that in the next role where it really mattered, my client would be prepared with new skills to handle this kind of situation?

If you're dealing with a difficult situation at work that's making you feel like you have no option but to leave, ask yourself: Is there a valuable lesson or other bigger purpose the discomfort is serving? Is this role a stepping-stone role for you along the path to your career purpose?

Ultimately, there is no job worth sacrificing your health and well-being to stay in for long, which makes it important to identify a "break-even" point so that you are clear what the boundary is between your situation being a learning opportunity and being downright unhealthy. If you feel that your situation is nearing the latter, develop a plan so that if you reach it, it will be clearer that it's time to leave and easier to do so. If you are in a prolonged, toxic situation that is compromising your physical or mental health, you may need to consider prioritizing your health over your paycheck after seeking appropriate advice.

✳   ✳   ✳

Your career purpose journey is what I like to call a "long game." Had I not stayed in some of the more difficult roles that I had, and instead simply looked for all-pleasant work, I would not have the experience and passions that I bring to my work today that helped me find meaningful work and enabled me to coach others through difficulties in their journeys. Try asking yourself what this step on your path might be trying to teach you, so that you don't "jump ship" too soon. As you can probably see by now, there is an important balance to strike between the latter and staying in an unfulfilling role indefinitely while fear holds you back from work you're meant to do. My hope is that, throughout this section, you've been able to weigh both sides carefully so that you can find the balance between fear-based stagnancy (or delay) and missing opportunities by acting too quickly.

What about you? Are there any assumptions you might be making about your dream job(s), whether they are included above or not? Where do you currently find yourself on a spectrum between wanting to leap abruptly to being paralyzed by fear? Is there any other preparation that you need, information that you should consider, or discussions that you should have with supporters, mentors, coaches, or professional advisors to ensure you've tested your assumptions?

FINAL THOUGHTS

If you run into roadblocks in this transition process, remember the story from chapter three in which I thought I had "failed" to go into the role and industry of my dreams after a year of unsuccessful interviewing. Keep in mind as you continue that, sometimes, our perceived failures are actually course corrections guiding us to exactly where we belong.

If you're struggling to find success in this transition time, try being curious about what this perceived "failure" is trying to show you. Take a step back and reconsider your options. It is absolutely in no way, shape, or form, a sign that you should stop trying. Ask your supporters for ideas, go back through alternative paths from the work that you did in chapters three through five, cycle back through the process (especially following your leads), ask yourself what you're not considering, or take a walk in nature to clear your head—anything to keep going. *Like the water in a creek that has encountered a rock in its path, nothing should stop you from continuing to flow beyond your obstacles.*

> Like the water in a creek that has encountered a rock in its path, nothing should stop you from continuing to flow beyond your obstacles.

If you've done your due diligence to set yourself up for success, consulted with loved ones and professionals, and find that fear is the *only* thing holding you back, then I say to you again: Life is too short not to go after your dream job. There's no need to rush the process, but that's also not a license to delay it because you're listening to your fears.

Lastly, remember to *enjoy* the process—whether or not the path is linear, you *are* on the path to the life of fulfilling work you are meant to do. I can think of few things that are more worth celebrating and enjoying than that!

What about you? Where can you start on the next steps that you have identified through this chapter? What other logistical steps do you need to take to make responsible changes toward getting your dream job? Is anything keeping you from going after it at this point? If so, what is the next step you could take to address it?

*   *   *

As you continue to follow the path along your career purpose journey, the most important thing to remember is to keep following your leads. Each dream job along your path will be unique and will require you to cycle through parts of this process. Your supporters will be with you throughout the journey, and this book will always be here as a resource for you. Should you ever feel alone on this path, please remember: *I* believe in you. I wouldn't have written this book otherwise.

When you find your dream job, tell us all about it! You can find more information at www.CareerPurposeBook.com. You never know whom your story will inspire, and I personally cannot *wait* to hear from you. Until that time comes, our final chapter together will give you some resources to help you if the path gets tough along the way.

CHAPTER 7
WHAT TO DO IF THE GOING GETS TOUGH

"Now I see I will never find the light unless,
like a candle, I am my own fuel."
— *Bruce Lee*

A few years ago, when I was on my last trip down the stairs before departing for a three-hour drive to teach in another state, it happened: I fell down the stairs. I was wearing shoes with inadequate grip on the soles, stepped on the edge of the carpeted stair instead of square in the middle of it, and the next thing I knew, my right ankle was twisted in an unnatural way and I was on the floor wondering what had just happened.

After I gathered myself and assessed the damage, my options for how I could respond included a range of anything from crying (or yelling) at my misfortune to calling and regretfully canceling my workshop facilitation duties. However, in that moment, I decided to believe something different.

There's this strange phenomenon that seems to happen throughout my life wherein something seemingly "bad" happens right before I'm about to do something good in the world. Call it whatever you want based on your belief system—fate testing us, Murphy's Law, spiritual warfare, etc. Whatever it was, it was in that moment when I sat dazed on the floor that I decided this was not only part of the path, but I took it as a sign that I was on exactly the right track. After all, if I wasn't out to do good in the world, what would there be about me to "fight" against? I smirked, stood up cautiously, and muttered to whatever this was: "Nice try. I can teach sitting down." I proceeded to complete the drive, and iced my ankle at the hotel that evening while listening to some music and preparing my flip chart visuals for the next morning's workshop.

You, too, have the power and perspective to see any roadblocks that you face—whether physical, mental, emotional, or spiritual—in a positive and productive light. The decision to go after your career purpose is a truly powerful message to everyone around you that you aren't messing around. You're no longer playing small, you know you're meant for more, and you're becoming who you're meant to be. When any challenges arise, you can show them that they're messing with the wrong person and triumph over them. You can have peace of mind knowing that it is an expected, natural part of the path to finding your career purpose (and life in general) to encounter obstacles. In fact, you can know that their presence is sometimes a sign that you're doing exactly what you're supposed to be doing, which makes it oddly comforting in a way.

You may be wondering at this point: does the journey *have* to be hard? The answer, of course, is no! I am by no means saying that. You have the full power to decide the journey will be easy and fun, and to manifest that reality. (I'd much rather you have that experience.) Remember that magical, little word *how* that we discussed adding to your thoughts to move past excuses? The same applies here—ask yourself *how* the journey could be easier or more fun, or how you could have *both* fun *and* deep transformation. It is, after all, important to enjoy the journey.

> Facing any limiting beliefs and fears you have is a natural part of the career purpose journey.

That said, as we discussed in chapter one, I've found that the underlying reason that people typically are not living their career purpose is that they are held back by limiting beliefs and fears, whether they are consciously aware of them or not. That means that, as you start going after your purpose, you may have to face them—and that is easier for some than it is for others. It is a natural part of the journey, and not only can you work through them but you can also leverage any challenges that you encounter in your path to help you thrive.

If you don't currently feel held back by limiting beliefs and fears, I'd recommend that you continue reading so that you know what's in this chapter if and when you need it. Once we get deep into the process, most of my coaching clients are surprised at just how much of the reason why they haven't acted previously is accounted for in those limiting beliefs and fears. A book on the traditional job-searching process all but certainly would not contain a chapter like this one, since you don't have to involve feelings to move to the next logical step in a career trajectory. Accordingly, you may not see until you get deeper into the process why this chapter is here; it is unique to a journey of purpose and fulfillment. Sometimes, that comes with other deep discoveries, and because we are all unique, each person's experience varies. *If* the process of facing any fears and limiting beliefs that you have becomes difficult for you, then this chapter is here for you when the going gets tough.

What about you? How will you choose to view any challenges that you encounter along the path to your career purpose? Take a moment to reflect on that so that you can make a positive decision proactively; you may recall from earlier that this means you'll be more likely to act accordingly when the time comes.

CAN WE *REALLY* OVERCOME LIMITING BELIEFS AND FEARS?

Given that our limiting beliefs and fears hold us back from the fulfilling work that we were meant to do on this earth, the question of whether we can overcome them is therefore of paramount importance to answer. Since this book is published and you're reading it, I bet you can guess the punch line (yes, we can overcome them!), but in the process of digging deeper into how, I discovered some important truths that you may need to consider, especially if you are struggling with this part.

Starting with the common advice

If you find yourself struggling with limiting beliefs and fears at some point along this journey, start with the prevailing advice and see if it works for you. If you do an online search for how to overcome limiting beliefs (or attend a class on the subject, as I did), the suggestions that you'll find go something like the following: put highly specific language on what you're feeling; reflect on where the belief or fear is coming from or the first time you remember feeling it; then, repeat affirmations to yourself or write a letter to these beliefs (or to the child version of you who experienced them for the first time). Finally, make the choice not to let the belief hold you back, and re-read your letter or affirmations daily, or as frequently as necessary, to remind you of the truth. These exercises are sufficient for some, so by all means, start there.

If you try them and still feel held back, that's okay too. As I explored whether it was possible to overcome limiting beliefs and fears, I found that the story of Sisyphus, a king from Greek mythology, makes a great analogy for how the prevailing advice made me feel. As punishment for cheating death twice, Sisyphus was forced to push a huge boulder up a hill, which then rolled back down to the ground every time that it got close to the summit—over and over, for eternity. What a fate! In my opinion, the prevailing advice, for a couple of reasons, felt lacking in hope in a way similar to pushing a boulder up a hill over and over. First, we are unlikely to succeed at the "battle" *every* day (because we're only human), and therefore, on those days in which we don't succeed, we may add a feeling of failure to the list of what we're already going through. Second, the act of fighting against something expends much of the energy that we need to keep going. If we fight a battle against our fears and limiting beliefs every day, and then start the battle anew the next day, what energy is left in us to go on the journey, much less enjoy it?

Reframing the "battle"

When I took a self-defense class in college, the teacher explained a technique rooted in Jiu Jitsu in which we should go *with* the energy of the opponent, not against it. This throws off the attacker, who is expecting you to resist their energy as you fight back. For instance, if they yank you by your arm toward them, the teacher said to go *with* them and adapt from there, instead of pulling back in the opposite direction as the attacker expects. This got me thinking: what if we could apply this tactic not only to a physical opponent, but also to our limiting beliefs and fears? What if we could reframe the nature of the "battle?"

Buddhist master Mingyur Rinpoche recounts a similar strategy in his story of how he overcame his panic attacks by doing what he calls "becoming friends" with his panic instead of defaulting to panic about the panic (or fear of the panic). Listening to him speak about this approach reminded me a lot of that Jiu Jitsu technique. I pictured us noticing the fears and limiting beliefs (that bubble up when we go after our career purpose) appearing next to us, tempting us to panic. Then, instead of freaking out about their presence or fighting them back as they arise, what if we said something like: "Hey there, I see you're here. Want a cup of tea? No? Okay then, I'm going back to what I was doing."[39]

> When we align our efforts parallel to our fears instead of fighting directly against them, we are empowered to keep moving forward.

When we reframe the nature of the battle this way—that is, when we align our efforts *parallel* to our fears instead of fighting directly against them—we are empowered to keep moving forward. We free up the energy we would normally be using to fight those battles, and we are then able to redirect that energy into our path and goal.

Asking better questions

Many of the people I've worked with found that the strategies above sufficiently helped unblock what was holding them back. However, I've also seen many cases where these strategies simply were not enough. If you've tried the techniques above and still feel held back, you're not alone. When I reached this point in my exploration, I was still determined to find "the" answer for all.

> The key is not in finding "the" answer to overcoming limiting beliefs and fears, but in the act itself of relentlessly trying new tactics until you find the one (or the combination) that is uniquely fitted to you.

And then it hit me: I was asking the wrong question. There is *an* answer, but the answer is not the same for everyone. Going back to our Sisyphus analogy, if your boulder keeps rolling back down the hill, then you haven't yet found the strategy that keeps your muscles strong enough to hold it up. *Thus, the key is not in finding "the" answer to overcoming limiting beliefs and fears, but in the act itself of relentlessly trying new tactics until you find the one (or the combination) that is uniquely fitted to you.* If you remember nothing else from this chapter, please remember that one statement.

Because we are all different and complex, some people need more unique or intense measures than others. On this journey, there are *so* many more options for help than we may realize at first—anything from a quick online search and printing some positive quotes, to deep work on the unconscious mind with a trained professional, and everything in between. If you find that the standard strategies don't resonate with you or don't help to unblock your path, ask yourself: What else is out there that you haven't yet tried? Where else can you look—books, online classes, apps, coaches? Who is further along on their path, or seems to be thriving, that you could ask how they did it? Could you try a different methodology? Could you try a nontraditional or holistic approach? How might any religious or spiritual beliefs you have come into play, and are there mentors in those communities you could talk to? What about talking with a licensed therapist? How could you reframe the approaches that you have tried in a new way—perhaps trying different affirmations, or on a different schedule, or with different people? Could you combine two or more approaches in a "recipe" tailored just to you and your needs?

I've seen a broad spectrum of needs in this area across the people I've worked with. On one end, some go on this journey successfully with just a bit of encouragement or by incorporating a few new, positive habits into their routine. On the other end, some are more intensely held back and may struggle greatly, often without feeling like they can pinpoint why. Where on this spectrum do you currently find yourself?

Just as we saw earlier that nobody can do the work to find your career purpose but you, it is also true that nobody can know exactly what you need but you, or do the work to find the solution(s) that work for you, or apply and practice the solutions, or overcome these beliefs and fears—but *you*. Wherever you currently are, there is hope and light ahead on your path; all you must do is never give up on the search for your unique needs.

That's right, reader, you *can* overcome your limiting beliefs and fears, and you will, but only if you go on the relentless pursuit to do so.

I can make this statement with confidence and integrity because I've lived it myself. There is no "do as I say, not as I do" here. Was it easy or quick to figure out? Did the first strategy I tried work? Of course not. What worked is that I made the unwavering decision to overcome my own limiting beliefs so that I could help others do the same; opened my mind to new possibilities (as we saw in the newspaper study from chapter two); and kept trying strategy after strategy, no matter how far "out of the box" they were, and doing the work that they each required, until I found the combination that finally worked for me. Through a couple of "chance" meetings, just the right coaches and books, and pure willpower, I unblocked my path, and so will you. Who knows where the answer will be for you when you just commit to keep looking!

> You can overcome your limiting beliefs and fears, and you will, but only if you go on the relentless pursuit to do so.

Don't hesitate to try new and different strategies if you feel like Sisyphus with his boulder. It doesn't matter if you need a unique, expensive, free, intense, unusual, easy, hard, or common solution, or some combination of all of the above. All that matters is that you find the one(s) that enable you to keep moving on the journey.

Lastly, as with most things in life, there is no point in time at which you are magically and permanently free from all new struggles forever. And that's okay—it makes the journey more interesting and gives us more opportunities to grow. Therefore, we must *all* keep exercising our proverbial muscles, through the strategies uniquely tailored to each of us, so that our muscles remain strong enough throughout our lives to keep our "boulders" at the top of our hill. It is in keeping these proverbial muscles strong that we bring our best, most authentic selves to the world, by unblocking our ability to effectively carry out our purpose.

What about you? Do you currently feel held back by limiting beliefs and fears? How much might they be affecting you, whether you've realized it before now or not? (If you're struggling to answer these questions, you could start by reflecting on why you haven't fully gone after your career purpose yet.)

If you haven't yet found the strategy for overcoming limiting beliefs and fears that works best for you, what two to three ideas do you have for next steps that you could take to pursue new ones or combinations? Whom could you contact for support or ideas?

If you don't currently feel held back, are there any strategies that you might want to make a note of to look more into later, should the need arise as you go deeper into this journey?

LET'S GET SOMETHING STRAIGHT:
YOU ARE ALREADY ENOUGH

The most common limiting belief among the people I work with is "I am not enough." So, before we dive into some tools that you can use when the going gets tough, I want to address that one belief directly. If you, like many, are experiencing some variation of the belief that you are not enough, I invite you to consider the following bigger picture questions:

To paraphrase a famous quote by Marianne Williamson: "Who are you NOT to be enough?" She also said, "Your playing small does not serve the world ... we are all meant to shine." No one else on Earth has your exact same talents, and no one else shares the exact same passions that you hold. You are not only enough, you are a rare and priceless treasure. What good does it do the world if you keep this treasure hidden? Even if it were possible that you weren't "enough," would the act of keeping your talents and passions hidden from us somehow *make* you enough?[40]

> "Your playing small does not serve the world ... we are all meant to shine."
> —*Marianne Williamson*

What about this: if you're not enough now, will there ever be another version of you that *is* enough? There's only one of you in all time— in the entire past, present, and future of humanity. Even within your own lifetime, is there some milestone that you can hit at which you are suddenly enough? What does "enough" mean for you—can you actually define it?

To dive deeper into this last thought, I looked up the word *enough* in various online dictionaries. The main idea that emerged among them was the idea of a "sufficient degree to fully meet a certain purpose." If we apply this to your career purpose, at what point do you have enough within you (that is, a sufficient degree) to fulfill *your* purpose? Who decides when you've met the criteria "adequately?" What is that threshold at which you suddenly become enough?

As you've probably guessed by now, I don't believe that there is one.

I ask these questions because their answers can help us see the arbitrary limits we place on ourselves that hold us back from living fulfilling lives, or worse, from feeling that we *deserve* to live fulfilling lives. Sometimes, simply noticing these limits—and their false or illogical narratives about us and our value—is enough to move past them.

You may not have enough certifications, credentialing, or other practical criteria in place to go after your dream job tomorrow, but the truth is that on a fundamental level, you are already enough.

The question is, will you choose to believe me?

A coaching client once told me that she at least believed that *I* meant it and would lean on that until she believed it for herself. It's completely fine if that's as far as you can get right now; as we discussed, the key is to make sure that you just don't stop until you *do* believe it for yourself.

TOOLS TO TRY IN DIFFICULT TIMES

Now that we've explored the truth about our obstacles, limiting beliefs, fears, and how we're already enough for the journey, I want to share a few tools that I've found helpful that you can try if the going gets tough. Because our limiting beliefs and fears risk stalling us, I wanted to provide you with a "menu" of options for any time you need a boost or a new strategy on a difficult day to make sure you keep going.

Even if you're not currently in need of one of these ideas, reading through them now will allow you to recall some on the fly when and if you do need them, and to know which parts you may need to come back to later. Therefore, as you read, I encourage you to note which two to three resonate the most with you, and whether there is anyone you know who may be struggling and could use some of these tips. We all need support sometimes, whether we're on the career purpose journey or not!

When you feel fear, choose faith instead

Recall the story I told at the beginning of chapter six in which I decided that I wanted people to tell the version of my story where I went after my dream job without hesitation. Will you make the same choice with whatever is standing between you and your dream job, and choose faith over fear? (To clarify, I'm not necessarily talking about religious faith but rather a belief that everything will work out.) During the moments when you feel fear, do you focus on the truth and the bigger picture, or do you have "blinders" on and struggle to see the situation for what it is?

In these moments, try taking a deep breath and reflecting on what's really going on. You're not in imminent danger of being eaten by a predator. What are you really afraid of, and what's the worst that could happen? Will this situation that you're facing matter in five months or five years?

Often, what we find is that our emotion exceeds the appropriate level for the risk, and this realization gives us the freedom and ability to choose faith over that fear. It is in those moments that faith reminds us that we will ultimately be okay. We then have the courage to act in spite of fear because we want to live a life of meaningful, fulfilling work *more* than we want the feeling of safety (or whatever perceived benefit our limiting beliefs and fears have given us).

> We gain the courage to act in spite of fear the moment that we want to live a life of meaningful, fulfilling work *more* than we want the perceived feeling of safety.

Visualize the people who need you to do what you're meant to do

Who stands to miss out if you don't live your career purpose? Who are the customers or the audience you will serve in your dream job, and what do they stand to lose if you don't go after it? One of my coaching clients has a dream of teaching English overseas. I suggested that he visualize the children sitting in his future classroom and what their lives would be like without his passion and gifts. In your case, you could give the people who need your gifts a name or personality—think about them as real people (because they are). If you're struggling to believe their lives would be all that different without you, another approach would be to visualize someone in your life who had the impact on you that you're trying to make in the world. In my client's case, I suggested that he visualize the best teacher he ever had and what *his* life would have been like without that teacher. The cost becomes too great not to act when we realize someone out there (or, more likely, many "someones") needs us to live out our career purpose.

Get a coach, an accountability buddy ... or better!

One approach that you could use is to work with a coach. As one myself, I can tell you we are happy to be your accountability buddy and cheerleader on your journey. You could also call a member of your list of supporters, tell them what your goals are and by when you want to accomplish them, and ask them to check in with you about those goals (or let them know when to expect an update from you about your progress). Better yet, get a copy of this book for them and encourage them to find and live their career purpose with you—so that we can *all* enter the path toward meaningful work, together!

Here's where this idea gets more interesting: If you go on this journey with someone else, you will actually enjoy the experience more. While it may be intuitive that shared experiences are more enjoyable, there's also research to prove it. A friend of mine told me about a study in which two participants ate chocolate at the same time, and then rated their experience. Despite being in different rooms where they neither interacted with nor could see each other, they reported increased focus, were more likely to report being on the same wavelength as the other person, and reported that the chocolate tasted better and more flavorful.[41]

As I was writing this book, I sometimes put on a shared music platform where I could listen to the same song with dozens of total strangers with whom I had exactly zero interaction and will never meet. I can personally vouch for how it made the music and my writing process more enjoyable just by knowing that others were listening to the same song "with" me and that I was not alone in that moment.

I hope it is equally meaningful to you to know that there are, at any given time, others reading this exact same book who are on the same career purpose journey as you (even though you may never know who they are). If you're looking for additional ways to get connected, I invite you to learn more at www.CareerPurposeBook.com.

Pay close attention to what you're telling yourself

As we learned in chapter two, we have the ability to manifest outcomes that we desire by focusing on what we want to happen. Often, when we are struggling, we can tune into our inner dialogue and find ourselves listing out all of the things that we don't want, what we're afraid of, what we worry might happen, or negative opinions that we fear others might have of us. You *do* have the power to turn this around, and that power starts with noticing what it is that you're telling yourself or focusing on. If you find yourself thinking these kinds of thoughts, take back the "driver's seat" and say the opposite to yourself; for example: I *can* do it, of course they'll love me, I *am* enough, and I *will* make it, and so on. Your mind is an extremely powerful tool in this journey—why not use it to your advantage?

Reward yourself to develop more positive habits

In *The Power of Habit: Why We Do What We Do*, author Charles Duhigg breaks down the components of the habit loop: the cue, the habit, and then the reward. Something cues us to do whatever the habit is, and then we get some sort of reward for that behavior. New habits do not form unless we not only *have* a reward to work toward (or identify what the reward was that we had been getting from the bad habit that we want to replace) but also, more importantly, *crave* that reward.[42]

Can you name a less healthy habit that you have formed and a more positive one that you wish to replace it with? Even something as simple as updating one aspect of your morning routine habits (such as getting up when your alarm goes off instead of hitting the snooze button) can have lasting effects on your stamina and demeanor throughout the day. Whether you choose to reward yourself with a piece of chocolate, a trip to your favorite spot, a relaxing evening, or a little "retail therapy," rewards can be helpful hacks for forming new, healthier habits to get us back on track in difficult times.

Feel the feelings, wean off the escapes

When negative feelings arise (and we all have them!), it is a common and understandable coping mechanism to want to suppress them. We may numb them through a variety of distractions or fight against them as we talked about earlier in this chapter. However, fighting, numbing, or distracting won't serve you well in a process of transformational change like your career purpose journey. They can take away your focus, prolong the journey unnecessarily, or serve as a reason not to keep trying. What can you try instead?

You may have heard the quote by Robert Frost, "The best way out is always through," but if that sounds a little daunting, it may be easier than you think. Did you know that the physiological lifespan of an emotion in the body and brain is only *ninety seconds*? No matter what you're feeling, sometimes simply allowing yourself to pause and focus directly on that feeling can be a rather efficient way of getting through it.[43,44]

As you continue on this path, it will be helpful to gently wean yourself off any escape mechanisms that you may be using so that you can face the journey, and any feelings that arise because of it, more directly. What is your escape of choice—scrolling through social media? Losing yourself in a novel? Binge-watching shows? Zoning out on a video game?

One of my coaching clients enjoyed reading fiction in her free time, but upon discussion in our sessions, she realized that it was actually an escape mechanism—a way for her to temporarily forget the frustrations of life that we all experience. She was committed to the journey and wanted to lean less on her novels as she worked through the process. In her case, reading was also one of the strengths she had identified. Because strengths are crucial fuel for the journey, she came up with the idea to switch to non-fiction. That way, she could be fueled by the activity without "escaping" into a story, which then provided her the clarity and time to focus more directly on finding her career purpose.

Note: If you think that you may have an addiction such as alcohol as your escape mechanism, please consult a professional for advice. This book is not intended to be a substitution for medical or other professional advice.

Instead of going around or fighting against the obstacle, make it a catapult

If you're struggling with an obstacle in your path—whether it's internal or external, big or small—and, if you haven't yet read *The Obstacle Is the Way* by Ryan Holiday, I would recommend making that your next read. It's a small but mighty book that will show you all the power and perspective that you have to turn your obstacle into a catapult toward success. One of the gifts that this book, which is based in the ideas of stoicism, gives the reader is a reminder of just how many things truly are in our control. Here are some examples: your attitude, how you react, what you focus on and what you ignore, what you decide to do, whether you give up or keep going, your perspective, and whether you choose to see the good in the situation (the list goes on).[45]

To embark on a challenging path is to, well, find challenges. You may have difficult days where you feel that you aren't good enough, that you can't find the right job, don't think you have what it takes, aren't successful fast enough, feel like the world is against you, and so on. Again, to have these feelings is normal, and you can still find meaningful work despite them. It is in those moments that you have the power to choose to focus on what you can control so that the obstacle in your path becomes not just something you can get around, but a catapult that you can use to launch directly into your career purpose.

You have the sole power to choose how you will act and feel and how you let the situation affect you. We all have challenges, setbacks, twists, turns, and unfairness in life. That is expected. The question is: What will you do with them when they arrive? (There are tons of great examples in Holiday's book, if you need some inspiration on where to start or if you want to see how others have navigated this mindset.)[45]

Now is the time to choose to focus, with unwavering determination, on the goal so that when these obstacles arise, you are expecting them and have a plan for how you use them to your advantage. If nothing else, there are always lessons to be learned, no matter how difficult the situation you encounter is. And yes, even your dream job will include difficult people and situations, so this mindset is an excellent habit to develop now.

Check in on your self-care

In chapter two about how to set yourself up for success, I mentioned that this is a whole mind, body, and spirit journey. Take a moment to check in on each of those areas. Are there any that you've let slip? Are you getting proper nutrition, water intake, exercise, and sleep? Are you active in your religious or spiritual life with prayer or meditation? Do you have adequate "me" time, family time, and resting time? I encourage you to give yourself grace and take care of yourself along this journey. I've seen how something even as simple as adding more protein to one's diet or a consistent bedtime have *major* effects on energy levels that can help us get through the obstacles.

When we're depleted, it can be hard to see how to make positive changes, so just remember that little magical word we talked about: *how*. *How* can you enjoy some physical activity *and* watch the kids? Maybe you can do something active together. *How* can you get a little more rest—even if it's just five minutes—in between commitments? Maybe you can shut your door, mute your devices, and set a timer. *How* can you get more steps in *and* get the errands taken care of? Maybe you can park a little farther from the door. With a little extra thought, or by asking a supporter to help us brainstorm, we *can* solve these challenges.

Act on positive ideas before wasting energy on judging or prioritizing them

If you're struggling, and a positive idea comes into your mind about something you could do, don't think about it—just do it without judging the idea or spending mental resources trying to prioritize it. If the name of someone on your list of supporters comes to mind, there's no need to spend any mental energy deciding if they're the right person to talk to; there is risk in stalling at that step, because your energy is already depleted in this state. Just reach out to the first person who occurs to you and ask them to remind you why they believe in you. If you start to think things like "I will feel more like doing that when I've had my coffee in the morning," "It doesn't make sense to travel that far," "I don't have the supplies I need to do that yet," or "There's no guarantee that will work," you may experience "decision fatigue" and not have the mental resources left for doing the very action that is likely to help you.

Keep your focus on the immediate next step if the whole journey is too daunting

I recently found a note that I wrote to myself shortly after I quit my job to start my business that I have no memory of writing. In short, it expressed a feeling of overwhelm and doubt as I looked at what I called the "mountain" of work that I had ahead of me to make it as a new business owner and the lack of a clear path to get there. If you relate to this feeling, I would love to share the wise words of one of my amazing coaches. I can hear her now: "Ashley, you're focusing on the size of the mountain. Where do you *start?*" The timeless advice to complete a journey, "like eating an elephant—one bite at a time," is critical in times when you find it to be too daunting.

When we're struggling or overwhelmed on our journey, it can sometimes be hard to see what those first steps are and to take the first one. As the late Reverend Dr. Martin Luther King, Jr. said in part: "[I]f you can't run then walk, if you can't walk then crawl; but whatever you do, you have to keep moving forward." If you're at a point where all you can do is "crawl," that's okay! Just starting somewhere—anywhere—will give you momentum. Once you make that first move, no matter how small, the rest become easier as your confidence grows.[46]

A fellow entrepreneur friend of mine once said, "If the question is whether to do the thing or not, the answer should always be do the thing." In other words, make the phone call. Send the message. Purchase the service. One small win is still a win! What is one bite-sized, next step you could take now?

> "When you want something, all the universe conspires in helping you to achieve it."
> — *Paulo Coelho*, The Alchemist

Harness the power of transferrable confidence

Sometimes, when you complete a goal (even a small one) that you didn't previously feel like you could, it gives you a sense of confidence that you "have what it takes." It also proves to you that, if you can complete that one goal, then you can also complete another. The sense of confidence that you feel can be transferable, which means that you could accomplish a goal in another area of your life and feel that transferable confidence on your career purpose journey.

For example, if you aren't particularly active, the feeling that you get when you run your first mile (or kilometer), or when you complete your first 5K, can make you feel like you can do anything—not just accomplish fitness goals—and give you just the boost that you need to keep going. If you feel stuck in your career purpose journey, what might be an attainable goal in another area of your life that you could try this week?

Keep reminding yourself of the bigger picture

Why did you start reading this book? What did you envision when I asked you what a career purpose meant to you, or what your ideal workday would look like? Revisit those notes, surround your work area with them, and go back to the image that you had of where you're going. You *will* manifest these dreams if you choose to, so it's time to start feeling excited accordingly. Don't wait—feel it now! It's already happening around you, anyway. You're reading this book and have probably already put some of the ideas into practice, so go ahead and feel the dream that is aligning for you on your path. Setting up a positive environment around you, as we discussed in chapter two, is a big part of this. If you haven't done so already, put a few reminders around you of the joy that is arriving in your life, such as a quote or image that reminds you where you're headed.

> You *will* manifest these dreams if you choose to, so it's time to start feeling excited accordingly.

Remember to lean on your supporters

Last but not least, one of the most powerful tools that you have when the going gets tough is one that you've already developed—your list of supporters. They care about you, want you to succeed, and are happy to hear from you. Don't hesitate to contact them.

YOU'RE ON THIS JOURNEY FOR A REASON

As we near the end of our time together in this book, I want to remind you that no matter how you feel each day on the path to your career purpose, where you are located on it, or how fast you are going, you are on it for a reason, and you're exactly where you're supposed to be.

I wish that I could personally coach every single one of you reading this book so that I could hear your amazing, unique story and encourage you directly. Even though I may not know you, thinking about you and your career purpose journey is the one thing that kept me going on the harder days of this writing process. You have already come so far, and there is still so much more ahead. I hope that you have found the overall process to be as helpful as if we were working together directly, and whether we do at some point or not, I would be remiss if I didn't leave you with a few of my favorite coaching questions to help reorient you to the reasons why you're here.

> You're exactly where you're supposed to be.

Sometimes, the right question can serve as just the trigger that you need to jumpstart you out of times of struggle or stagnation on the path (accordingly, some of the questions below are similar in wording in hopes that one resonates). Select a few that resonate with you:

- What do you stand to gain when you're living your career purpose? How will it improve your life and the life of others (your family, friends, colleagues, classmates, customers, etc.)?
- What do you stand to lose if you don't embark on—or continue on—the journey to find your career purpose?
- What will the effect on others be if you don't go after your career purpose? What would the world miss out on?
- What is it costing you to stay where you are? What is it costing those around you?
- What would an impactful mentor (current or past) or a loved one tell you to do?
- What advice would you give to a friend facing your current situation?
- Is there anything else that you feel you need right now? What's the first step that you could take toward getting what you need?
- Which is worse: living to pay the bills, or taking some risks to find fulfillment? Why?

- If, heaven forbid, you found out you had a week to live, would you feel that you had done all you could in life? What could you do differently now in order to feel that way?
- Imagine you are sitting at a nursing home in your final years of life, reflecting on the life you've lived. What regrets do you have? How could you prevent these regrets now?
- How might the decisions and path you choose now impact your future, the future of your friends, family, and colleagues, or your legacy?
- What remaining hesitations do you have, if any? What does the "wise person inside" say that you should do?

As always, feel free to process these questions in the way that best serves you, whether that's through journaling, reflection, or in discussion with a loved one or supporter. Notice as you work through them if you experience any changes to your perspective or feelings and what you should do as a result.

FINAL THOUGHTS

Keep trying the strategies throughout this chapter. Keep talking to different supporters or coaches. Keep attending classes, webinars, reading books, or doing *whatever* it takes until you find your "ah-ha" moment in the way that *you* need to hear it.

Don't settle for the affirmations that someone else recommends if they don't work for you. Don't be afraid to invest time or money into healing yourself or growing and progressing on your journey—you and your well-being are priceless! Most importantly, don't give up or fall for all the reasons that you should.

So what if you have to tell your same story to ten different therapists ten different times before you find the one you "click" with? So what if you need to spend a little more time or money in order to find out if one particular strategy or coach works for you? So what if the right solution for you is inconvenient, hard to figure out, or complicated to implement?

If that's what it takes for you to overcome what's holding you back, then that's what it takes. You have to just keep trying things. No excuses, remember? Do not stop looking until you find what keeps your "muscles" strong. Your story, your career purpose, and those of us in the world around you who need you are counting on you.

You deserve to live your best, most uninhibited life, dear reader. Only *you* can manifest that reality, and only you know what you need along the journey.

As the quote at the beginning of this chapter so wisely stated, you are your own fuel. You already have the power within you to keep going, to keep believing in yourself, and to keep going after your career purpose. You are self-sufficient, complete, and worthy of joy.

And in case nobody has told you lately, or you need to hear it again, you are enough. You have always been enough, you will always be enough, and the value that you bring to this world is *limitless*.

Now, go get that dream job.

CONCLUSION
YOU NOW HAVE A RESPONSIBILITY TO ACT

"If you don't build your dream, someone will hire you to build theirs."
— Tony Gaskins

Now that you know how to find and live your career purpose, you have a *responsibility* to act. You can no longer make the excuses that you used to make, nor let your fears or limiting beliefs keep you from acting. The world *needs* you and your gifts.

The easiest course of action that you could take after you read this book would be to do nothing. Please don't tell me that I wrote a whole book just for that outcome! Why not go for it? What do you *really* have to lose, when you think about the last day of your career or life and the feeling that you'd have if you didn't go after it?

My hope is that this book has helped to clarify your path and to remove any roadblocks preventing you from embarking on it. I hope that you can now clearly see how the costs of not going after your career purpose are worse than any risks it takes to get there. The world has everything to gain from you giving us your fullest, most authentic self, and everything to lose if you don't.

When (not if) you are in your initial dream job, the journey doesn't end there. You'll grow and change, as will the job and the people you serve in it.

Just keep following those emotional leads proactively throughout your time there so that, as your dream job changes along your career purpose path, you are ready to make the next leap.

You don't have to be famous or make it into textbooks to make a life-changing imprint in this world. The impact and inspiration that you can have within your own inner circle of friends and family will be immense, and possibilities that you had no idea existed will come to fruition as you continue on this journey.

> "Excitement comes from the achievement. Fulfillment comes from the journey that got you there." — *Simon Sinek*

The level of joy that you'll experience by living your career purpose only comes from a place of having conquered your fears and doubts. In the moment when you realize that you are living your career purpose, it will mean immeasurably more than it would have if the path had been an easy one. The fulfillment, then, comes from the journey, and often from the hardest struggles along the way.

As you continue on this journey, I have a few final words of encouragement. First, I hope that you will appreciate each of the lessons that you learn along the way, even though some are more costly (monetary or otherwise) than others. They are all important parts of the process, even if some lessons are harder to learn than others. Second, focus on the joy that you will feel at each milestone along the way to help keep you going. Just as the saying "Rome wasn't built in a day" suggests, progress takes time, effort, iteration, and stamina. Give yourself some grace, and remember: if it weren't hard at times, it wouldn't be as joyful in the end. Lastly, remember to enjoy the process! Celebrate your successes, focus on the bigger picture if you reach a perceived failure, and when you're living your career purpose, please pay it forward at every possible opportunity.

What excuse do you have left?
Do it tired.
Do it scared.
Do it discouraged.
Do it unprepared.
Do it alone.

Do it hurt or heartbroken.
Do it without complete information.
Do it despite constant interruption.
Do it if you don't feel that you have enough time or money.
Do it if you don't feel like you're ready.
Do it when the timing isn't "right."
Do it when you don't know how to start.
Do it if you think that you don't have everything you need.
Do it if you feel like nobody else believes in you but me.

However you feel, you must do the work, and you must do it without hesitation. We're never fully "ready," and there will always be an excuse not to act. You're the only one who can decide that you will go on the journey and do the work that it requires along the way. None of us is guaranteed tomorrow. The world needs you—and the most uninhibited expression of your gifts and passions—in it. It doesn't need them later or someday. It needs them now. Today.

* * *

May we all find and live a life of fulfilling work, because life is too short to live any other way. More importantly, may we encourage one another on this path. I urge you to help reveal your loved ones' unique contributions too. If you found this book helpful, please share it with them. Let's build a world in which we all live our career purpose; learn more on our website at www.CareerPurposeBook.com.

READ THIS WHEN YOU'RE IN YOUR DREAM JOB

Because I have full confidence that you will one day soon be in your dream job, I wanted to include a couple of thoughts for you to read when that time comes:

Periodically look back at your notes from this process
When you get exactly what you hoped for, it can be surprisingly easy to forget how much you once wished for what you have now. I still keep some old appointments on my calendar to remind myself just how much more joyful my situation is now and how grateful that I am to be in the place I worked so hard to get to. Looking back on your notes from this process can remind you, too, how far you've come and how much you have to be proud of.

Give back and pay it forward
To whom do you attribute your success, and have you thanked them properly? Whose list of supporters can *you* be on now? Whom do you know who is a few steps behind you that you could mentor? Have you encouraged anyone else to find and live their career purpose? May we always pay forward the kindness of those who have helped us along our path.

Remember to take time for yourself and your loved ones
Just because you love what you do and may never want to stop, doesn't mean that you shouldn't—and just because you no longer need a vacation to "escape" doesn't mean that you shouldn't still take one. Celebrate life, get plenty of rest, and enjoy even the smallest moments with your loved ones!

Get your story out there

You have a unique path, a story that nobody else has, and a way of talking about it that nobody else can. People *need* to hear it! However you share it—whether via interviews, talking with friends and family, or writing your own book—please get your story out there to inspire others to find and live *their* career purpose. You never know who needs to hear your story. Whether it inspires them, motivates them, or gives them a feeling of permission or courage to face their challenges, you can change someone's life in a way that nobody else can.

Update us on your journey

Get in touch at www.CareerPurposeBook.com so that we can celebrate you and your success. You earned it, and I personally can't *wait* to hear all about your career purpose journey!

Above all, CONGRATULATIONS!! I knew you could do it, or I wouldn't have written this book. I am already so deeply proud of you and your work on this path before I even know who you are. May you continue to enjoy every day of the journey.

Wishing you a lifetime of fulfilling and meaningful work,
Ashley Freeman

WANT TO GET INVOLVED?

HELP US CREATE A WORLD IN WHICH WE ALL LIVE A LIFE OF FULFILLING AND MEANINGFUL WORK!

Gift a copy to a friend, associate, or family member

If you have found this book to be valuable and know others who would find it useful, we encourage you to consider buying them a copy as a gift. Special bulk discounts are available if you would like your whole team, audience, or organization to benefit from reading *The Path to Your Career Purpose*. Please contact Info@CareerPurposeBook.com or visit www.CareerPurposeBook.com for more information about bulk orders.

Share your review

Your rating will help other readers know that this is the right book for them. Let's help more people find and live their career purpose! Would you consider giving this book a rating wherever you bought it? Online bookstores are more likely to promote a book when they feel good about its content, and reader reviews are a great barometer for a book's quality.

We invite you to consider visiting the website of wherever you bought the book, search for Ashley Freeman and the book title, and leave a review. If you are able, consider adding a picture of you holding the book, which increases the likelihood that your review will be accepted.

Work with Ashley and her team

Ashley accepts a limited number of speaking and coaching engagements each year. To learn how you can bring her message to your organization, please contact Info@CareerPurposeBook.com or visit www.CareerPurposeBook.com.

Learn more

Our website includes even more ways to get involved!
Visit us at www.CareerPurposeBook.com to learn more.

ACKNOWLEDGMENTS

This book truly took a community to make it happen. Without the stories, examples, guidance, and support from so many people, there would be no book. Accordingly, any words I could write here feel insufficient, but I will do my best to capture the significance of everyone's contributions and beg for forgiveness where any part may be incomplete.

First, to my family—Wes Freeman and Cheryl Sroka—who read my manuscript multiple times, gave innumerable helpful suggestions that sometimes even turned into entire paragraphs or sections this book wouldn't otherwise have, endured the many complaints (sorry!) about how hard the process was, took care of daily needs while I was locked away writing for months on end, and encouraged me along the way . . . I owe you an eternal debt of gratitude.

To my editorial board members, Michael Doyle, Cathy Fyock, Elizabeth Ruth, Mary Rachel Henderson, and Christine Zhou, the quality and quantity of your feedback was priceless to me. I want every reader of this book to know how much we all owe you for the time that you took to carefully read and comment. You helped me see not only which parts were great and should remain intact, but also where concepts were not clearly explained, needed more examples, were redundant, or needed a shift in tone. As a result of your comments, the manuscript grew by 33 percent in length, and more importantly, light-years in clarity!

Thank you to my book coach, Cathy Fyock, without whom I would have had no clue how to go about writing a book or the structure and community support to make it happen, and to my publishing team, Everett O'Keefe, Malia Sexton, and Chris Simmons, who made the publishing process efficient and easy to understand.

I also want to thank those who graciously allowed me to provide their examples and stories throughout the book, whether through an interview

(Jason Bell, Shyla Esko Bare, and David Papa), responding to my LinkedIn posts (Jeff DeGarmo, Jeremy May, Aaron Morrison, Raye Perez, and Diane Sarjoo), encouraging me to celebrate writing milestones and to find joy in every day (Maureen Sweatman), helping me unblock my writing path through discussion and coaching about limiting beliefs (Alex Yoel and Aaron Morrison), or by graciously allowing me to quote them or use examples from their journeys (Mark Castille, Michael Fox, Ehren Gruber, Mary Rachel Henderson, Elizabeth Ruth, Heather Tunison, and Emily Twa).

To the many people who encouraged me along the way, your role may have been the most important. In addition to those mentioned previously, I want to thank the members of the No Stress Book Club, the members of Cathy Fyock's weekly author forum, the Ynternational [With a WHY] community (thank you especially to Angel Lovecchio for sharing the research study about shared experiences), my social media followers who responded to all my posts throughout the process, and to the countless individuals who signed up for book-related updates, voted on the cover art design, asked me how the process was going, answered my requests for input, and reminded me on the harder days how much the world needs to hear these ideas.

To Danielle Rubenstein and Brandon Smith, I would never be where I am without your coaching, mentorship, and encouragement throughout the years. Danielle, thank you for sharing your insights and expertise as a career coach, and for your encouraging words that appeared multiple times throughout the manuscript through story. Brandon: I couldn't possibly do justice to a thank-you here. There was nobody more perfect to write the foreword for a number of reasons, and your generous support without hesitation over the years of my journey to find my career purpose is one of the main reasons that I am here today.

Lastly, to all those who believe in the vision described in this book and are working to help spread the word, *you are* the movement. Without you, I could never reach the people outside my immediate network who need to hear this message. Here's to a day when we all know our career purpose, have the courage to go after our dream job, and live the life of fulfilling work that we were meant to do.

ENDNOTES

1. "Finding Happiness at Work," Jenna Goudreau, March 4, 2010, *Forbes*, https://www.forbes.com/2010/03/04/happiness-work-resilience-forbes-woman-well-being-satisfaction.html. Accessed Jan. 28, 2022.

2. "On the Rise of Shareholder Primacy, Signs of Its Fall, and the Return of Managerialism (in the Closet)," Lynn A. Stout, Winter 2013, Cornell Law Faculty Publications, Cornell Law Library, https://scholarship.law.cornell.edu/cgi/viewcontent.cgi?article=2310&context=facpub. Accessed Jan. 28, 2022.

3. "Is the Great Resignation BS? Statistics show it's not all that," Workplace Evolution, Jay L. Zagorsky, *The Conversation*, Fast Company & Inc., 1/13/22, https://www.fastcompany.com/90712286/is-the-great-resignation-bs-statistics-show-its-not-all-that. Accessed February 17, 2022.

4. "The Great Resignation," Felix Richter, Jan. 11, 2022, U.S. LABOR MARKET, Employment in the United States, Statistica, Statistica.com, https://www.statista.com/chart/26186/number-of-people-quitting-their-jobs-in-the-united-states/. Accessed February 17, 2022.

5. "These Are the Top 5 Reasons People Are Quitting During the Great Resignation, According to a Massive New Analysis (Hint: None of Them Is Pay)," Jessica Stillman, Jan. 2022, *Inc.*, Inc.com, https://www.inc.com/jessica-stillman/great-resignation-mit-revelio-research.html. Accessed February 17, 2022.

6. Susan Cain, *Quiet: The Power of Introverts in a World That Can't Stop Talking* (Crown, 2013).

7. "Manage Your Energy, Not Your Time," Tony Schwartz and Catherine McCarthy, Burnout, *Harvard Business Review*, 2007.

8. Aliya Alimujiang, MPH; Ashley Wiensch, MPH; Jonathan Boss, MS; et al., "Association Between Life Purpose and Mortality Among US Adults Older Than 50 Years," May 24, 2019, JAMA Network, American Medical Association, https://jamanetwork.com/journals/jamanetworkopen/fullarticle/2734064. Accessed Jan. 28, 2022.

9. "Will a purpose-driven life help you live longer?" November 28, 2019, Kelly Bilodeau, MIND & MOOD, Harvard Health Publishing, Harvard Medical School, https://www.health.harvard.edu/blog/will-a-purpose-driven-life-help-you-live-longer -2019112818378 and National Library of Medicine, NIH, https://pubmed.ncbi .nlm.nih.gov/?term=(Kim%2C%20Eric%20S%5BAuthor%5D)%20AND%20 (purpose)&sort=. Accessed Jan. 28, 2022.

10. "Psychology: Your Attention, Please," Michael Blanding, *Princeton Alumni Weekly*, https://paw.princeton.edu/article/psychology-your-attention-please. Accessed Jan. 28, 2022.

11. David Allen, *Getting Things Done: The Art of Stress-Free Productivity* (Penguin Books, 2002).

12. "What Impact Does the Environment Have on Us?," Mary Jo Kreitzer, RN, PhD, 2016, Regents of the University of Minnesota, https://www.takingcharge.csh.umn .edu/what-impact-does-environment-have-us. Accessed Jan. 28, 2022.

13. Ulrich, R.P., Quan, X., Zimring, C.P., Joseph, A., Choudhary, R. (2004). "The Role of the Physical Environment in the Hospital of the 21st Century: A Once-in -a-Lifetime Opportunity." *The Center for Health Design, September 2004,* https://www .healthdesign.org/system/files/Ulrich_Role%20of%20Physical_2004.pdf. Accessed Jan. 28, 2022.

14. Greenwald, A. G., Klinger, M. R., & Schuh, E. S. (1995). "Activation by marginally perceptible ("subliminal") stimuli: Dissociation of unconscious from conscious cognition." *Journal of Experimental Psychology: General,* 124(1), 22–42. https://doi.org/10.1037/0096-3445.124.1.22

15. "What is NPS? Your ultimate guide to Net Promoter Score," Qualtrics.com, Qualtrics, https://www.qualtrics.com/experience-management/customer /net-promoter-score. Accessed Jan. 28, 2022.

16. Don Miguel Ruiz and Janet Mills, *The Four Agreements: A Practical Guide to Personal Freedom (A Toltec Wisdom Book)* (Amber-Allen Publishing, Incorporated, 2018).

17. "Defining Strengths," Marcus Buckingham, Jan. 29, 2020, TMBC, https://www.marcusbuckingham.com/defining-strengths. Accessed Jan. 28, 2022.

18. "Spend a Week in Love with Your Job," Marcus Buckingham, April 17, 2019, TMBC, https://www.marcusbuckingham.com/spend-a-week/. Accessed Jan. 28, 2022.

19. Stephen R. Covey, *The 7 Habits of Highly Effective People: 30th Anniversary Edition* (Simon & Schuster, 2020).

20. "Mini-Mastermind Series: Stress & Meditation Uncovered with expert Gianna Biscontini," 16:10, May 12, 2020. https://www.facebook.com/DesignYourDetour/videos/664161294367740/.

21. "Multitasking: Helpful or Harmful?" McGraw-Hill Higher Education, November 9, 2018, McGraw Hill, https://www.mheducation.com/highered/insights-ideas/multitasking-helpful-or-harmful.html. Accessed Feb. 16, 2022.

22. "Multitasking Damages Your Brain And Career, New Studies Suggest," Travis Bradberry, October 8, 2014, Leadership, *Forbes*, https://www.forbes.com/sites/travisbradberry/2014/10/08/multitasking-damages-your-brain-and-career-new-studies-suggest/?sh=5fb5079e56ee. Accessed Feb. 16, 2022.

23. Hilton, L., Hempel, S., Ewing, B. A., Apaydin, E., Xenakis, L., Newberry, S., Colaiaco, B., Maher, A. R., Shanman, R. M., Sorbero, M. E., & Maglione, M. A. (2017). "Mindfulness Meditation for Chronic Pain: Systematic Review and Meta-Analysis." *Annals of behavioral medicine: a publication of the Society of Behavioral Medicine*, *51*(2), 199–213, https://doi.org/10.1007/s12160-016-9844-2.

24. van der Riet, P., Levett-Jones, T., & Aquino-Russell, C. (2018). "The effectiveness of mindfulness meditation for nurses and nursing students: An integrated literature review," *Nurse Education Today*, *65*, 201–211, https://doi.org/10.1016/j.nedt.2018.03.018.

25. Bargh, J. A., & Morsella, E. (2008). "The Unconscious Mind." *Perspectives on psychological science : a journal of the Association for Psychological Science*, 3(1), 73–79. https://doi.org/10.1111/j.1745-6916.2008.00064.x

26. Gollwitzer PM. "Implementation intentions: Strong effects of simple plans." American Psychologist. 1999; 54:493–503. http://kops.uni-konstanz.de/bitstream/handle/123456789/10101/99Goll_ImpInt.pdf?sequence=1&isAllowed=y. Accessed Jan. 28, 2022.

27. "The Luck Factor," Richard Wiseman, Skeptical Inquirer, May/June 2003, http://richardwiseman.com/resources/The_Luck_Factor.pdf. Accessed Jan. 28, 2022.

28. Patterson et al., *Crucial Conversations: Tools for Talking When Stakes Are High, Second Edition* (McGraw Hill, 2011), p. 12–16; *Washington Business Journal*, May 2005; Daniel Dana, *Managing Differences: How to Build Better Relationships at Work and Home*, 2005, 4th ed. (MTI, 2006); Barbara J. Kreisman, "Insights into Employee Motivation, Commitment and Retention," Feb. 2002.

29. Jen Sincero, *You Are a Badass at Making Money: Master the Mindset of Wealth* (Penguin Publishing Group, 2018).

30. Dr. Bessel van der Kolk, *The Body Keeps the Score: Brain, Mind, and Body in the Healing of Trauma* (Penguin Publishing Group, 2015).

31. "Two Parts of the Brain Govern Much of Mental Life: Understanding the roles of the amygdala and the prefrontal cortex," Jeremy Shapiro, PhD, Nov. 5, 2021, *Psychology Today*, https://www.psychologytoday.com/us/blog/thinking-in-black -white-and-gray/202111/two-parts-the-brain-govern-much-mental-life. Accessed March 6, 2022.

32. Daniel Goleman, *Emotional Intelligence: Why It Can Matter More Than IQ* (Random House Publishing Group, 2005).

33. Marcus Buckingham and Ashley Goodall, *Nine Lies About Work: A Freethinking Leader's Guide to the Real World* (Harvard Business Review Press, 2019).

34. Thomas Edison, "Failure Quotes," Goodreads.com, Goodreads, Inc., https://www.goodreads.com/quotes/tag/failure, Accessed March 29, 2022.

35. Simon Sinek, David Mead, and Peter Docker, *Find Your Why: A Practical Guide for Discovering Purpose for You and Your Team* (Portfolio, 2017), https://simonsinek .com/product/find-your-why/.

36. Daniel Coyle, *The Culture Code: The Secrets of Highly Successful Groups* (Bantam, 2018).

37. Robert B. Cialdini, *Influence: The Psychology of Persuasion (New and Expanded)* (Harper Business, 2021).

38. "Managing Yourself: Turn the Job You Have into the Job You Want," Amy Wrzesniewski, Justin M. Berg, Jane E. Dutton, From the Magazine (June 2010), Harvard Business Review, https://hbr.org/2010/06/managing-yourself-turn-the -job-you-have-into-the-job-you-want. Accessed Jan. 28, 2022.

39. "How A Tibetan Buddhist Master Dealt With His Panic Attacks," Susannah Gruder, https://www.huffpost.com/entry/how-a-tibetan-buddhist-master-dealt-with -his-panic-attacks_n_57d2bdcfe4b06a74c9f426cf

40. Marianne Williamson, "Quotable Quote," Quotes, Goodreads.com, Goodreads, Inc., https://www.goodreads.com/quotes/928-our-deepest-fear-is-not-that-we-are -inadequate-our. Accessed March 29, 2022.

41. Boothby, Erica J., Margaret S. Clark, and John A. Bargh, "Shared Experiences Are Amplified," Yale University, *Psychological Science*, 2014, Vol. 25(12) 2209–2216, © The Author(s) 2014. Reprints and permissions: sagepub.com/journalsPermissions .nav DOI: 10.1177/0956797614551162, https://clarkrelationshiplab.yale.edu/sites /default/files/files/BoothbyClarkBargh(1).pdf

42. Charles Duhigg, *The Power of Habit: Why We Do What We Do in Life and Business* (Random House, 2012).

43. Robert Frost, "Quotable Quote," Quotes, Goodreads.com, Goodreads, Inc., https://www.goodreads.com/quotes/614381-he-says-the-best-way-out-is-always -through. Accessed March 29, 2022.

44. Jill Bolte Taylor, PhD, *My Stroke of Insight: A Brain Scientist's Personal Journey* (Penguin Books, 2009).

45. Ryan Holiday, *The Obstacle Is the Way: The Timeless Art of Turning Trials into Triumph* (Portfolio, 2014).

46. Dr. Martin Luther King, Jr., "Quotable Quote," Quotes, Goodreads.com, Goodreads, Inc., https://www.goodreads.com/quotes/26963-if-you-can-t-fly-then -run-if-you-can-t-run. Accessed March 29, 2022.

62215958R00102

ABOUT THE AUTHOR

After a seven-year journey to discover her career purpose, Ashley Freeman is living her dream as a full-time coach, facilitator, and entrepreneur. She wrote *The Path to Your Career Purpose* so that others can expedite the process toward living their dream, too.

In 2018, Ashley founded Flourishing Work LLC, a firm that serves both individuals and organizations through customized coaching and facilitation services. She and her team have a passion for helping people gain the clarity and interpersonal skills they need to make meaningful, intentional progress every day toward their best selves. She has coached hundreds of individuals, from early career professionals to senior leaders, and has facilitated workshops on a variety of interpersonal and leadership topics for dozens of corporate and nonprofit organizations throughout the years.

Ashley holds an MBA in leadership from Goizueta Business School of Emory University, a BA in French with a minor in music from Emory College of Arts and Sciences, and she is a Myers-Briggs® Master Certified Practitioner. *The Path to Your Career Purpose* is her first book.

In her free time, Ashley serves as a volunteer coach for U.S. Military veterans transitioning to civilian careers. She also enjoys teaching cello and piano lessons, traveling, crocheting, and spending time with her family.

You can reach Ashley at Info@CareerPurposeBook.com or find more information at www.CareerPurposeBook.com.